CONTENTS

INTRODUCTION

"Money is made in Guayaquil and spent in Quito." So goes the traditional saying which typifies the division between Ecuador's two main cities. A division between the hot, humid, and bustling port of Guayaquil and the cool, sedate mountain city of Quito. A division between a commercial hub and a seat of government, between entrepreneurs and administrators. A division which shapes many aspects of Ecuador's daily life and which has largely shaped its tumultuous history.

Rivalry between the two cities is legendary. *Quiteños*, the capital's inhabitants, mock Guayaquil people as coarse and uncultured, as *monos* (apes) surrounded by banana plantations. *Guayaquileños*, on the other hand, disparage the capital as a cold, dull place, far from the beaches and full of bureaucrats. In the nineteenth century such animosity fueled the almost constant wars between rival political factions, struggling to control a divided nation. With its history of religious foundations, conservative landowners, and military leaders, Quito was the antithesis of liberal, free-trading Guayaquil. While Quito was the city of tradition and aristocracy, Guayaquil was home to generations of migrants and traders, more interested in money than nobility.

If today such distinctions linger on, other more serious divisions have come to characterize Ecuadorean society. Its indigenous population, long treated as serfs by wealthy landowners, are on the move, demanding land, rights, and respect. A recent wave of mobilization has taken traditional politicians by surprise and reasserted indigenous identity. In the Amazon region, home to some of Ecuador's indigenous communities, a bitter environmental battle is raging, pitting oil companies against local inhabitants and activists. As Ecuador markets itself as the region's main eco-tourism destination, there are concerns over the destruction of its rainforest by foreign oil companies.

This book aims to explain the factors behind Ecuador's conflicts, both ancestral and modern. It traces the development of a society split by geography and culture, of a nation often at war with its neighbors. It looks at a country whose natural beauty is under threat, where oil has been as much a curse as a blessing. It also examines the renaissance of Ecuador's four million indigenous people and explores their contribution to a rich and distinctive culture.

1   HISTORY AND POLITICS: BORDERING ON WAR

In January 1995 war suddenly broke out in the remote Cordillera del Cóndor in southern Ecuador. A border dispute between Ecuador and neighboring Peru which had been simmering for years erupted into full-scale violence. As Ecuadorean troops shot down Peruvian aircraft and helicopters and Peruvian infantry streamed into Ecuador, some thousands of troops were mobilized on both sides. Special taxes were levied to finance the war and people living in the border regions were evacuated. Ecuador's president at that time, Sixto Durán Ballén, declared that he would not yield a single inch and demanded a just settlement. His Peruvian counterpart, Alberto Fujimori, declared a ceasefire after several Ecuadorean frontier posts were said to have been taken.

After a month's fighting which claimed some 100 lives, diplomatic consultations proceeded sluggishly, the real grounds for the conflict lost amid a welter of nationalistic rhetoric and sporadic border clashes. Ecuador, it was calculated, had spent more than $900 million on the war with its more powerful neighbor. Some believed that the real motive was the promise of oil fields in the disputed territory; others maintained that Ecuador's goal was eventual access to the Amazon River through its network of tributaries. Meanwhile, popular feeling was reflected in slogans on the walls of Quito: *"Perú, Caín de Latinoamérica'*; "Peru, Cain of Latin America," a biblical reference to the murder of Abel by his brother Cain.

There are those in Ecuador who maintain that the rivalry between their country and Peru dates back to the time of the Incas. In 1532 the Inca King Atahualpa, with the aid of a mighty army of Indians from the region of Quito, defeated his half-brother Huáscar, the ruler of Cuzco in south Peru. Centuries later, although modern nation states have replaced kingdoms, animosities persist.

The Fall of the Kingdom of the Incas

When the great Inca king Huayna-Cápac died in 1527, his kingdom split into two parts. The north was ruled by Atahualpa, the son born of his marriage with Paccha, the daughter of Carchi, who was leader of the powerful Quitucara people living in and around what is now the city of Quito. In the south, power fell into the hands of Huayna-Cápac's son Huáscar, born of another union with an Inca princess from Cuzco, the ancient Inca capital. Atahualpa marched on the south with his Quitucara army and defeated his half-brother, whom he then proceeded to murder along with the whole of his family. He became the new sole ruler of the Inca kingdom. Shortly afterwards, Francisco Pizarro, the Spanish adventurer, landed with 180 troops on the coast near the site of the modern town of Túmbez. An exploratory expedition under Bartolomé Ruiz had already visited the area around Esmeraldas six years earlier.

An Inca kingdom had already existed from the eleventh century, situated in southern Peru around Lake Titicaca. It was not until the fifteenth century, after 1438, that the Incas began to expand their immense empire under their leader Yupanqui and his son Túpac-Yupanqui. At that time there was a chain of small kingdoms in the Andes of modern-day Ecuador; the largest were those of the Quitucaras in the north and the Cañaris in the south. The Cañaris, living around Cuenca, resisted the incursions of the Incas with considerable determination, entering into an alliance with neighboring communities. Together they concluded favorable peace terms with the Inca king Túpac-Yupanqui in about 1470. The Quitucaras succeeded in resisting the Incas for more than another twenty years.

Valdivia Culture

Valdivia statue

Tony Morrison/South American Pictures

The first inhabitants of Ecuador were hunters, fishers, and gatherers who probably lived in the Andes at least thirty to fifty thousand years ago. Gradually their way of life changed as agriculture developed and the first permanent settlements came into existence. The remains of what is termed Valdivia culture date from between 3500 and 1500 BC and have been found in the coastal plain. The sites of towns containing hundreds of houses, in which little earthenware figures have been excavated, are among the oldest in South America.

For a long time it was assumed that the Valdivias came from the Japanese island of Kyushu because of a striking similarity revealed by samples of earthenware. In recent years, however, the idea has been steadily gaining ground that the exchange of technologies and ideas between coast dwellers and inhabitants of the Amazon region was the basis of Valdivia culture.

The female figure was fashioned by hand and baked. Figures such as this have been found in great numbers, and it is not known whether they were broken deliberately. It is assumed that they were once used for magic healing and fertility rites.

Inca sun temple, Ingapirca   *Kimball Morrison/South American Pictures*

Although the Incas allowed the peoples they conquered a certain amount of cultural freedom, they nevertheless tried to impose their sun religion on the northern moon-worshipers. They laid waste to the strategically situated city of Ingapirca (to the north of Cuenca) and on its ruins built a sun temple and an astronomical observatory. Huayna-Cápac, the son of Túpac-Yupanqui, was born in Tomebamba, the modern-day Cuenca, and was of Cañari descent. In Ingapirca he established one of his temporary residences. Once Huayna-Cápac had extended the Inca kingdom in the south by the addition of parts of northwest Argentina and northern Chile, he turned his attention to the obstinate Quitucaras.

Quito was captured in 1492 and became a garrison town from where the Incas made further inroads into the north. The Quitucaras, however, continued to resist and only after twenty years of struggle were they subdued. The northernmost frontier of the Kingdom of the Incas then lay beyond the Colombian city of Pasto. Yet the conquest still did not bring calm and stability, which came only when Huayna-Cápac made Quito his residence and married the daughter of Parchi, the captured Quitu leader. Their son was Atahualpa.

The Sword and the Cross

Having consolidated his power over the whole kingdom, Atahualpa established his capital in the city of Cajamarca in northern Peru. It was towards Cajamarca that Pizarro and his 180 *conquistadores* marched southwards from Túmbez. Although suffering from the heat and disease, the small Spanish company made steady progress, crossing mountain ranges and finally reaching the fertile upland valley of Cajamarca. The Indians regarded both the bearded men and their horses (they were unknown in the New World) as demigods and dreaded their superior weaponry. Worse, the war between the two brothers had left the once monolithic Inca kingdom critically weakened.

In order to break the Incas' resistance the conquistadores devised a trap with which to get rid of the popular Atahualpa. A Spanish priest was sent to convert the Indian leader to Christianity, and when Atahualpa, angrily rejecting the imposition of an alien religion, threw the priest's bible to the ground, he was overpowered by Pizarro and his men and taken prisoner. Atahualpa offered the Spaniards enough gold and silver to fill his cell in exchange for his freedom, but the offer was to no avail. Despite receiving over twenty tons of gold and silver, Pizarro held Atahualpa prisoner and, accusing him of adultery and of the murder of his brother Huáscar, had him baptized and strangled. His followers exhumed his body in order to rebury it in a secret place near Quito. Atahualpa is still a potent symbol for Ecuador's *indígenas* or Indian population, who honor him as a hero and who wait in secret for his return.

From Cajamarca the Spaniard Sebastián de Benalcázar set off for the north in 1534 to conquer Quito, then ruled by Atahualpa's general, Rumiñahui. When Rumiñahui received the news that the conquistadores were on the march, he opted to destroy Quito before the Spaniards could take the city. On December 6, 1534, after intense fighting, Benalcázar founded the city of San Francisco de Quito on the rubble of the destroyed city. Within fifteen years the conquest of the territory which today belongs to Ecuador was complete and was given the name Real Audencia de Quito, the Royal District of Quito. Approximately two thousand Spaniards had subjected half a million Indians to their rule. In the process tens of thousands of Indians had lost their lives.

Spanish Rule and the Struggle for Independence

The Spanish conquest of Ecuador was fueled by a gold rush. Rumors and myths circulated that to the east of Quito there was a *país dorado*, a land of gold, and various expeditions were organized to the Amazon region. The most important was the suicidal foray led by General Francisco de Orellana, who in March 1541 set off eastwards with 350 soldiers and 4,000 Indians in search of gold. The expedition was completely unprepared for the perils of the tropical rainforest and was stricken by the debilitating climate. Not until a year after his departure did Orellana reach the Atlantic coast with

Quito, c 1620

Courtesy of Tony Morrison/
South American Pictures

fifty surviving men. Although he had found no gold, he was the first European explorer to cross South America from west to east.

Because the Amazon was opened up from the city of Quito, Ecuador continues to consider that it has historical claims on free access to the Amazon River, coining the slogan *"Ecuador País Amazónico,"* "Ecuador, country of the Amazon." Peru, however, maintains that Orellana started his expedition from Cuzco, entering the Amazonian forest via Loja, Cuenca, and finally Quito.

Serfdom and Forced Labor

As elsewhere in their American colonies, the Spanish introduced into the Audiencia de Quito the *encomienda*, the feudal agricultural system whereby the Indians were assigned to a Spanish landowner on whose land they lived and for whom they were forced to work. In exchange, he was in theory obliged to see to their needs, protect them, and provide them with the assistance of a priest who could teach them the faith of the Roman Catholic church. The Indians, the *encomendados*, were allocated a piece of infertile land on which they built their *choza*, a hut of earth and reeds, and cultivated a little food for their own use. The Indians received a pittance for their work and were almost always in debt to their landowner or *encomendero*. Their children inherited the accumulated debt, ensuring the continuance of the system. The Indians did not accept this exploitation passively, and from time to time there were bloody uprisings.

At the end of the sixteenth century the *mita* was revived, a system which laid down a specific period during which Indian serfs had to work for landowners or other members of the colonial elite. The system had originally been introduced by the Incas, but was now adapted by the Spanish who forced craftsmen to work in *obrajes* or workshops. The introduction of the mita led to a massive growth of textile production in particular, and the Audiencia de Quito developed into one of the most dynamic industrial centers of the Spanish colonial empire.

The church played a decisive role in consolidating Spanish colonial government; large numbers of Indians were converted to Roman Catholicism and in the sixteenth and seventeenth centuries Quito, with its scores of churches and religious institutions, was the missionary center from which Jesuits and Franciscans set off for the Amazon. As a consequence, in 1642 the territory of the Audiencia de Quito was extended to the basin of the river Marañón in modern Peru, a process through which the church became the region's most important landowner.

Haciendas and Cocoa

After 1700 came a period of economic recession. The size of the Indian population had shrunk considerably as a result of forced labor and the many diseases which the Spanish had brought with them. In actual fact, the encomiendas had increasingly become private estates in which the landlord held complete power and the Indians labored as slaves. Natural disasters and volcanic eruptions also contributed to destabilizing agricultural and textile production. To turn the tide the Spanish set about confiscating large areas of land which were still in the hands of the Indian communities. An enormous expansion of large-scale land ownership came about in the form of *haciendas*, huge privately owned estates.

For the Indians whose land had been confiscated, there was little else to do but to start working for the landlords as *huasipungueros* under the same conditions as had existed during the encomienda system. In Quichua, the language of the Indians living in the Sierra, *huasipungo* means "at the door of the house" and refers to the piece of infertile land on which the serf's hut was built and where, if one was lucky, some crops might be grown. Not until the land reforms of 1964 did the remaining huasipungeros become independent farmers and escape their serf-like status.

In the eighteenth century the production and export of cocoa, the "golden bean," began in the tropical coastal plain. Because of the shortage of indigenous labor, slaves were imported from Africa to work on the plantations.

Towards Independence

In the second half of the eighteenth century unrest began to grow among the colonial ruling class who had been born in the American colonies. The *criollos*, as they were known, were frustrated by the overwhelming influence exercised by Spain over every aspect of economic and political life and resented the way in which newly-arrived Spaniards took the best jobs in the bureaucracy. Oddly enough it was the child of an indígena and a *mestizo*, Eugenio de Santa Cruz y Espejo, who was the first champion of independence in the Quito region. He paid for his courage with his life, but resistance to Spanish hegemony was brewing everywhere and the independence of the United States in 1776 was a source of inspiration.

Following Napoleon's invasion of Spain in 1808, the Spanish crown tried to tighten its grip on the colonies. On August 10, 1809 a group of criollos reacted by seizing power in Quito, demanding the abolition of Spanish trade monopolies. Troops were sent from Lima and Bogotá to restore Spanish rule, but succeeded only through widespread repression. It was not long, however, before a fresh uprising broke out, this time in the coastal city of Guayaquil, home of the powerful cocoa-producing and trading middle classes. Inspired by the war of independence which the Venezuelan general Simón Bolívar had begun elsewhere on the continent, a group of *notables* proclaimed independence in 1820. Led by José de Sucre, one of Bolívar's generals, a decisive battle on May 24, 1822 against the royalist army took place on the slopes of the Pichincha volcano which won a settlement in favor of the rebels.

In order to avoid territorial disputes, Bolívar decreed that the existing colonial borders had to be respected by the new states coming into being. The Audiencia de Quito, which since 1718 had been part of the Spanish Vice-Royalty of New Granada, therefore became a state of the Federation of Gran Colombia, which also included Colombia, Venezuela, and Panama. The Federation was not destined to enjoy a long life and it fell apart as early as 1830. For most Ecuadoreans Bolívar's visionary Federation had, in any case, been a source of resentment, subjecting them to military rule by Venezuelans and Colombians and taxes which went to Bogotá. Yet another Venezuelan general, Juan José Flores, married to an aristocratic lady from Quito, then founded the state of "Ecuador," taking its name from the findings of a French exploration party which in the eighteenth century had determined the exact position of the equator. In its report it spoke of *las tierras del Ecuador*, the "lands of the equator."

A few months before Gran Colombia disintegrated, the frontier between Peru and the Federation was laid down in the Mosquera-Pedemonte Memorandum. Notwithstanding Flores' insistence that the new state should have the same frontiers as the Audiencia de Quito, the declaration of independence merely noted that the new state comprised the departments of Quito, Guayas, and Cuenca. Peru maintained, on the other hand, that this did not constitute a continuation of the old colonial entity, rather that a new state with a new name had been created. Ecuador, in Peru's view, could no longer claim the borders as determined in law by the old Audiencia de Quito.

Liberals versus Conservatives

After independence the criollos won political power but were faced with the daunting task of welding together the three relatively isolated colonial departments into a single unit. In the central and northern Sierra, with Quito as its center, the conservative landowners and the Roman Catholic church were in charge; in Cuenca in the south, small farmers and artisans dominated but politically and economically the region was of little importance. On the coastal plain of the west were the cocoa plantations where the country's only export commodity was grown. This meant that the port and trading centre of Guayaquil achieved a strategic economic and political significance. By dint of their intensive contacts with the outside world the bankers, traders, and plantation owners of the coast took on the prevailing liberal ideas which came from Europe and North America.

The areas of conflict between liberals and conservatives all too soon began to determine politics. The former considered themselves champions of innovation, while the latter wished to perpetuate the colonial system. On the coastal plain, where in 1850 fewer than 100,000 people lived, work was scarce, but there was an abundance of fertile land suitable for agriculture. With an eye to expanding the cocoa industry, the liberals wanted to introduce wage labor in place of the huasipungo system so that the Indians could be moved to work on the plantations. The conservative estate owners of the Sierra were naturally vehemently opposed. Another point of conflict was trade; the liberals wanted to abolish almost all trade restrictions, but because free trade could lead to unlimited imports of textiles – which would undermine production in the Sierra – the conservatives were absolutely against it.

This ideological conflict dominated the country for the whole of the nineteenth century and spawned a succession of *caudillos* (strongmen) and intermittent bloody civil war. The army took alternate sides or itself seized power, with the result that in the first 95 years of independence 40 presidents, dictators, and military juntas followed one other. Ecuador became a byword for political instability and violence.

In 1859 internal disintegration had reached a low point: Guayaquil was governed by a general, Cuenca had proclaimed independence, Quito had a provisional government, and Loja declared itself to be an "independent federal territory." Deciding to capitalize on the chaos, Peru invaded, blockaded the port of Guayaquil and entered into negotiations with Colombia about dividing up the country. Eventually, however, the Ecuadoreans succeeded in expelling the invaders.

Catholic Tyrant

In 1861 the ultra-conservative and devout Catholic, Gabriel García Moreno, came to power, dominating the country's politics for almost fifteen years (1861-1875). Supported by the estate owners in the Sierra, the autocratic Moreno succeeded in transforming the country into a fundamentalist Catholic state in which those of other persuasions were persecuted. Only Catholics were allowed to teach and the contents of schoolbooks and newspapers were censored by the bishops. In a gesture of religious zeal,

Moreno even changed the name of the country to "Republic of the Sacred Heart of Jesus."

Ecuadorean refugees organized resistance to the Catholic tyrant from Panama and Colombia. One of these refugees was the liberal journalist, Juan Montalvo, whose books, with titles such as *The Eternal Dictatorship* were circulated underground in Quito. In 1875 Moreno was assassinated on the steps of the presidential palace. When he heard the news, Montalvo reportedly cried out in delight, "My pen has killed him!'

Liberal Revolution

After Moreno's death his supporters desperately tried to hang on to power, leading to the setting up of two parties organized on religious lines, an ultra-conservative party and a liberal-Catholic party designed to compete with the orthodox Liberal party. Within the Liberal party itself a division also took place, with the founding of a radical faction under the leadership of the former anti-Moreno guerrilla, General Eloy Alfaro, and a moderate wing.

Increased cocoa, coffee, and palm nut exports led to a period of rapid economic growth after 1880, meaning that the economic power of the Liberals in Guayaquil increased rapidly and the influence of the Quito Conservatives waned. A *coup d'état* in 1895, which brought the liberal and anti-clerical Eloy Alfaro to power, pushed the balance definitively in favor of the Liberals.

The "Liberal Revolution," which was to last until 1912, brought far-reaching changes. Eloy Alfaro's modernizing policies were designed to promote the economic integration of the country and to this end, with help from U.S. investors, a railway line was built between Guayaquil and Quito, a seemingly impossible undertaking in those days because of the steep terrain and enormous costs. In 1908 it was possible to travel from Guayaquil to Quito by train in twelve hours; before then the traveler would have needed twelve days.

High among Eloy Alfaro's priorities was a plan to reduce the power of the Roman Catholic church and to separate church and state. The Liberals particularly resented the fact that the church, as the most important land holder, owned huge tracts of prime land which were not used productively, and spoke of "property in dead hands." By means of the *Ley de Manos Muertas*, the Law of the Dead Hands, the land owned by the church was expropriated and distributed among smallholders. Alfaro also rescinded the church's sole right to teach, religious education was proscribed in the newly-founded state schools, and the government introduced civil marriage.

Various factors contributed to the crumbling of Eloy Alfaro's power. Seventeen years of Liberal government had not been able to alter the balance of power in the Sierra. Although the church's land had been seized, the power of the Conservative landlords and the oppression of the Indian population had continued as before. In the end, sectarian divisions among the Liberals proved to be Eloy Alfaro's undoing and in 1911 he was ousted by his own supporters. When a year later he tried to arbitrate between various Liberal factions, he was imprisoned and then murdered by a group of pro-Catholic soldiers whose slogan was *"Viva la religión y mueran los masones"*; "Long live religion and death to the freemasons." The Liberals nevertheless succeeded in remaining in power from 1912 to 1925.

Economic Crisis, Political Chaos

Due to the disruption of the First World War, international demand for cocoa fell dramatically and it was only after the Second World War that a recovery took place (crop diseases also played a part). Ecuador hence lost its principal source of export revenue while at the same time the price of imports rose, with the result that an economic crisis was inevitable. Consecutive Liberal governments adopted drastic austerity measures and large sections of the population suffered abject poverty. In the meantime, the landowners looked for alternative export products, which they found in the form of coffee, rice, and bananas.

Faced with increasing poverty, the plantation workers in the coastal region began to become organized and in Guayaquil they set up the country's first trade union, the Confederación Obrera de Guayas, which led militant strikes and demonstrations for better pay and conditions. In the Sierra the *peones* also revolted and demanded higher wages. On both occasions the protests were put down with bloody force. As the Liberal government gradually lost its hold on the country, the pressure for change became ever stronger, especially from the conservative *serranos* who blamed what they saw as a corrupt Guayaquil oligarchy for the country's woes. The end came on 9 July 1925, when a military junta assumed power without bloodshed. But stability did not return with the new government and the economy deteriorated still further. In 1932 *la guerra de los cuatro días*, the "four-day war," broke out, a civil conflict in which more than 4,000 people were killed as armed civilians and soldiers defended Quito against an army of Liberals from Guayaquil.

Velasco Ibarra and Military Politics

One man succeeded in capitalizing on the chaos: José María Velasco Ibarra. Originally a Conservative, he cultivated a populist rhetoric which managed to win over large sections of liberal opinion, with the result that in 1933 he

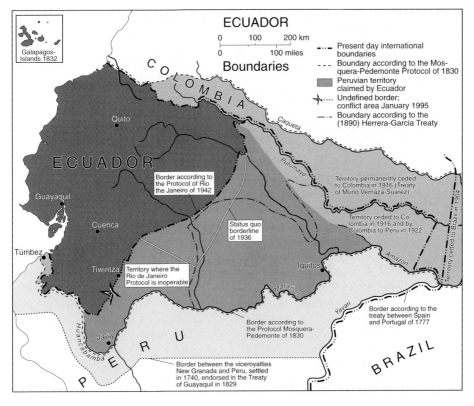

ECUADOR

Boundaries

was able to take power with the support of the Liberals. His political program was something completely new to a country used to the old two-party divide. His appeal lay in a strident personality cult, violent criticism of the rich and a proto-fascist taste for "morality," party discipline and street thugs. Most of the population, hungry for radical changes, lapped it up. Velasco was the prototype populist demagogue whose ideology was less important than oratory and charisma. He himself was well aware of his qualities and typical of his political persona was the remark, "Give me a balcony and I shall become president." In 1935 he dissolved Congress and proclaimed himself dictator. Almost immediately the army deposed him and he had to flee the country. The political chaos lasted throughout the 1930s, when in ten years there were no fewer than fourteen presidents.

The Peruvian Invasion

The border disputes between Ecuador and its neighbors, which dated back to independence, had, despite mediation by the Spanish crown in 1904, still not been settled. In that year Ecuador had accepted annexation of the most eastern part of its Amazonian territory by Brazil. In 1916 the border dispute with Colombia was settled by ceding a tract of Amazonian rainforest to the south of the rivers Caquetá and Putumayo. To the dismay of Ecuador, Colombia then gave some of this land to Peru in exchange for free access to the Amazon River.

Ecuador paid dearly for this settlement when, in 1941, Peru was able to launch another invasion from all sides. Within a short time most of the southern provinces of El Oro and Loja and a part of the Amazon region were occupied, a few towns in the south were bombarded and Guayaquil was blockaded. Such were his domestic political problems that the Liberal president of the day, Carlos Arroyo del Río, was powerless to repel the invasion, since his troops were garrisoned in Quito to suppress potential internal unrest.

Representatives from Chile, Argentina, Brazil, and the U.S., who were meeting in Rio de Janeiro in early 1942 to discuss the entry of the U.S. into the Second World War, added the Ecuador-Peru dispute to their agenda. The four countries agreed to act as guarantors for the implementation of the Rio Protocol, a treaty in which the borders between Peru and Ecuador were again defined. Under the terms of this treaty, Ecuador lost more than half its territory and the four countries threatened that if Ecuador did not accept the proposal Peru would be entitled to continue its occupation and would capture Guayaquil with no intervention on their part. The Ecuadorean delegation felt that it had been betrayed and brought the news home that "every country on the continent has left Ecuador in the lurch."

Velasco Ibarra organized the opposition to President Arroyo and the Liberal Congress which he held responsible for this disaster. In the wake of the "Protocol of Sacrifice" Velasco returned from exile and again came to power, this time at the head of a heterogeneous coalition of socialists, communists and conservatives. The coalition quickly disintegrated, whereupon Velasco once again proclaimed himself dictator; he was deposed in 1947.

A Confusing Border Quarrel: Two Tiwintzas

During the demarcation of the frontier in accordance with the Rio de Janeiro Protocol, representatives of the guarantor countries (Argentina, Brazil, Chile, and the U.S.) ran into a difficulties in the dense jungle. One problem was finding the exact location in the Cordillera del Cóndor of the watershed between the Río Zamora and the Río Santiago which was supposed to serve as the frontier. In 1947 American aerial photographs showed that between the two rivers there was in fact a third river – the Río Cenepa. The U.S. then presented both countries with a map showing a border arbitrarily determined, it seemed, by the Americans. In 1960 President Velasco Ibarro declared the Rio Protocol null and void. This declaration of *nulidad* found no support in the region, and the guarantor countries insisted that the Protocol had to be observed. Nevertheless, Ecuadorean jurists and politicians have since maintained the position of *nulidad* into the 1990s, and generations of Ecuadoreans have been brought up with maps showing the country in its pre-1942 borders. Around January 29, the date of the signing of the Protocol, skirmishes regularly take place in the Cordillera del Cóndor, where over a distance of approximately 48 miles there is no frontier demarcation.

In January 1995 the quarrel broke out again. After a few weeks of fighting both countries announced that they controlled the strategic garrison of Tiwintza, situated in the disputed territory. While President Fujimori claimed to have visited the settlement, the Ecuadoreans insisted that they had fought off a Peruvian attack. Tiwantza became a symbol of national pride, and Ecuador even accused Peru of building a new border post and calling it Tiwantza. By 1996, following a ceasefire, attempts began again to determine a definitive frontier line.

Peace and Bananas

With the arrival of the Liberal President Galo Plaza in 1948 came an unprecedented period of calm and political stability, the so-called "democratic parenthesis," which was to last until 1960. This stability largely reflected the economic growth resulting from improved cocoa and coffee exports and the flourishing banana industry. From representing a mere one per cent of exports in 1945, bananas came to provide two-thirds of Ecuador's export earnings by 1960, bringing renewed prosperity to coastal producers and traders.

In 1952 Velasco again became president on the basis of an aggressively populist program. On this occasion, he completed his period of office and after four years handed over the presidency to Camilo Ponce of the Partido Social Cristiano (PSC, the Christian Social Party), a splinter group of the Conservatives – but only temporarily. Velasco returned yet again to the presidential palace in 1960 by exploiting the anti-U.S. sentiments which were rife in Ecuador in the wake of the Cuban revolution. Velasco also promised his supporters all kinds of vague solutions for cranking up the Ecuadorean economy. The banana boom was beginning to falter after its peak in 1960, the government was faced with a drastic fall in revenue and was forced to cut spending. Social unrest again raised its head.

Enter the Generals

Velasco's promises came to nothing and, fearing that the Cuban revolution would spread to Ecuador, the army intervened in 1963. A military junta (1963-6) attempted to change the economic structure of the country, started an ambitious program of modernization and in 1964 announced land reforms. In this respect at least the military could rely on U.S. support, since Kennedy's Alliance for Progress advocated land reforms in all Latin

American countries in order to forestall a repetition of the Cuban revolution. In the following years, however, only a few farmers were able to benefit from the reform, as the agency in charge of its implementation struggled with lack of resources and money as well as against the entrenched interests of the big landowners.

The Ecuadorean military government was less repressive than those in neighboring countries, even though it reassured its civilian backers by inveighing against the evils of socialism and communism. The progressive student movement, in particular, became a target for the generals and the central university in Quito was closed.

The traders and bankers of Guayaquil, however, proved to be more powerful opponents and eventually they managed to apply economic pressure against the military. The generals withdrew and following a transitional period it was once again the aging Velasco who succeeded in winning the 1968 election. Student protests and economic mismanagement quickly undermined his administration and in order to head off a mounting crisis he resorted to a well-tried recipe, proclaiming himself dictator in 1970. With the support of the army he declared the constitution invalid and dissolved Congress, but within two years the military had had enough of him and removed him from the presidential palace.

The 1972 coup marked the end of the controversial figure of Velasco Ibarra who had been president five times between 1933 and 1972. His popularity with the poor majority did not always guarantee his political survival since on four occasions he was forced to resign and on three he declared himself dictator. Although he tried to establish a new political culture, he was never a serious threat to either the liberal or conservative elites whom he constantly vilified in his speeches. Yet the enormous popularity he enjoyed in spite of everything is demonstrated by the fact that since his death in 1979 his supporters still gather at his grave every year to pledge their allegiance to the cult of *Velascismo*.

The Military and Oil

The February 1972 coup had various motives besides removing Velasco. Firstly the military feared that the anti-militarist populist from Guayaquil, Asaad Bucaram, would win the 1972 elections and curtail their influence. Even more importantly, they were convinced that only they – and not corrupt politicians – were entitled to preside over Ecuador's new-found oil wealth. In 1967 large deposits of oil had been discovered in the Amazon region and after the dramatic global oil price rises at the beginning of the 1970s it was clear that the country had enormous potential wealth. Finally, within the military a group of progressive nationalists had come to the fore, arguing that the oil income had to be controlled by the state for the benefit of the country and not the traditional elites.

The Revolutionary National Government, as the junta called itself, promised radical modernization and far-reaching economic reform; oil extraction was placed under state control, foreign companies were forced to renegotiate their contracts, and an agreement, favorable to the government, was reached with Texaco to collaborate in exploration. In order to strengthen its position as an oil-producing country, Ecuador became a member of the Organization of Petroleum Exporting Countries (OPEC). Together with Colombia, Chile, and Peru, Ecuador also set up the Andean Pact with the goal of increasing regional free trade.

Very soon millions of petrodollars were flowing into the military's coffers. As well as oil revenue, the government sought extra capital through foreign loans, the aim being to establish a large-scale program of industrialization in order to reduce imports and diversify manufactured exports. The program never really got off the ground, however, and little came of the promised implementation of the land reform.

Most Ecuadoreans saw their high expectations frustrated amid growing rumors of corruption in military circles. By 1976 the more radical nationalist officers had been replaced in government by more conservative generals, willing to open the oil industry to foreign interests. As poverty rose again after the brief boom, unrest grew. The trade unions in particular, united in the Frente Unitario de Trabajadores (FUT, the United Workers' Front), orchestrated opposition to the military. The junta reacted by agreeing to hand over power to an elected government by 1978. During the latter years of the military administration political repression took increasingly harsh forms.

Democracy and Retrenchment

By 1979 Ecuador once again had a democratically elected government, thus marking the first military dictatorship in Latin America to return peacefully to barracks. A center-left coalition, with its power base in Quito, led by the youthful Jaime Roldós Aguilera, came to power. After years of military mismanagement and corruption, Roldós held out the prospect of technocratic reform, but events conspired against him. One central reason for the new government's failure was the opposition's majority in Congress, where Asaad Bucaram, once an associate of Roldós, led a campaign of obstruction and confrontation. But even more important were developments on the oil market and in the international financial world.

By the end of the 1970s Ecuador was already having difficulty in meeting the debt obligations it had contracted during the boom. In 1980 oil prices began to fall and in 1981 the international debt crisis broke. An economic collapse was inevitable since government expenditure by far outweighed oil income, and the economic situation deteriorated even further when in 1981 the border conflict with Peru flared up again. In the same year, moreover, the popular Roldós was killed in suspicious circumstances in a plane crash. His deputy, Osvaldo Hurtado Larrea, opted for drastic austerity measures and called in the International Monetary Fund (IMF) to arrange a rescheduling of the debt. The subsequent package of adjustment measures – cuts in subsidies, a devaluation of the *sucre,* and state-sector redundancies – gave rise to violent protests led by the FUT.

Andean Thatcherism

In the 1984 elections the centre-left was narrowly beaten by a centre-right coalition of Social Christians, Conservatives, and Liberals, the Frente de Reconstrucción Nacional (FRN, the National Reconstruction Front). The victorious presidential candidate was León Febres Cordero, a millionaire member of the Guayaquil elite and in many ways an old-fashioned caudillo, whose campaign style included arriving at meetings on horseback. Febres Cordero was an outspoken champion of the free market, and his program of neoliberal policies, likened to "Andean Thatcherism," in recognition of the British prime minister's drastic reforms, prioritized export-led growth, foreign investment, and a reduction in state intervention. Febres Cordero also cultivated close contacts with the U.S. Reagan administration which praised his free-market crusade and promised aid and investment.

But the social cost of Febres Cordero's neoliberalism was to prove high, and rising living costs sparked off a series of strikes. To head off such protests, he resorted increasingly to strong-arm tactics; according to Amnesty International, human rights violations became more widespread, while breaches of the constitution and conflicts with the judiciary were commonplace.

After 1985 problems mounted for Febres Cordero's government, as in September of that year oil prices again went into free fall, leading to even more retrenchment. In early 1986 Frank Vargas Pozzas, an air force general, made an unsuccessful attempt to take power and a few months later the FRN lost its majority in Congress to a center-left coalition. Febres Cordero's *macho* image then suffered a further blow when, having been kidnapped by supporters of the imprisoned Vargas, he immediately agreed to release the general, an act widely seen as cowardly. Then, in March 1987, northern Ecuador was struck by a serious earthquake. Hundreds of people lost their lives, 90,000 were made homeless, and for five months the Trans-Ecuador Pipeline was out of service, bringing oil exports to a standstill. Febres Cordero then suspended interest and capital payments on the foreign debt.

Borja supporters, Quito   *Julio Etchart/Reportage*

Ironically, the one-time favorite "model debtor" of the international banking community had no choice but to default on the country's $11 billion debt.

Borja and "Gradualismo"

Deeply discredited, the right lost the 1988 elections to the *Quiteño* Rodrigo Borja Cevallos and his newly-formed centre-left Izquierda Democrática (ID, Democratic Left), who also defeated the eccentric Guayaquil populist Abdalá Bucaram, the successor to Jaime Roldós and leader of the Partido Roldosista Ecuatoriano (PRE, Ecuadorean Roldosist Party). The elections turned once again on the classic opposition between coastal plain and Andes, with Guayaquil broadly representing free-market thinking and Quito the more traditional ideas of state intervention. Because of its rapid growth in population over the last 40 years the political weight of the coastal zone has increased accordingly, and since 1979 all victorious presidents had won a majority in Guayaquil. Interestingly, Borja's victory broke this pattern.

Borja distanced himself from the aggressive neoliberalism of his predecessor and pledged a program of social-democratic reforms, dubbed *gradualismo*. Economically, however, he had little room for maneuver, since inflation was running at an annual rate of 56 per cent and further debt renegotiations were due. Unpopular adjustment measures were inevitable. Politically, too, Borja was trapped, caught between the reformist expectations of the labor movement and the instinctive hostility of Guayaquil's industrialists, who viewed him a dangerous socialist. In a bid to balance these opposing pressures he introduced *concertación*, a consensus blueprint in which government, trade unions, and employers were supposed to reach agreement on policy-making.

Yet despite rising oil prices, Borja failed to lower inflation beneath 50 per cent, while rising unemployment and prices alienated the FUT which led a number of damaging strikes. Amid mounting social unrest, Ecuador's indigenous organizations also made their presence felt in a 1990 "uprising" which demanded guarantees to land and human rights (see Chapter 2).

Durán Ballén

In 1992 the center-left was swept away to make way for the center-right, led by the 72-year-old ex-mayor of Quito, Sixto Durán Ballén, who had failed to win the PSC nomination, forming his own Partido Unitario Republicano (PUR, United Republican Party). Thanks to his contacts with commercial leaders in Guayaquil and experience within the apparatus of government, he was the only candidate to have a reasonable level of support in both the Sierra and on the coast. Together with the Partido Conservador (PC, Conservative Party) of Alberto Dahik, who was appointed vice-president, he formed a coalition government, intent on rolling back Borja's reformism and reinvigorating neoliberal policies. In a return to the free-market theories of the 1980s Durán preached the virtues of modernization, decentralization, and, above all, privatization.

From the outset, Sixto Durán Ballén faced two insurmountable obstacles. First and foremost, practically every interest group, including the military, trade unions, and indigenous organizations, were opposed to his privatization plans. A proposal to amend the land reform law, which would have provided for the free sale of communal Indian land, met with fierce protests from indigenous groups and had to be gradually revised. In addition, his coalition only had eighteen of the 77 seats in Congress, a number halved after the 1994 legislative elections. Confronted by a hostile Congress, the president depended upon the grudging support of his former party, the PSC.

The ambitious privatization plans gradually ran into trouble, and few reforms actually materialized. Instead, Sixto Durán Ballén's government came under fire for alleged incompetence and corruption. Its nadir came in October 1995 when Vice-President Dahik fled to Costa Rica to escape arrest on corruption charges. What popularity Sixto Durán Ballén had gained from his jingoistic stance against Peru rapidly disappeared.

"The Madman"

As Durán's credibility plummeted, the outcome of the 1996 elections seemed predictable. PSC candidate, Jaime Nebot, was ahead in the opinion polls, followed by former Quito mayor, Rodrigo Paz of Democracia Popular (DP, Popular Democracy). Then, only months before the elections were due, a new political movement, Nuevo País/Pachacutec was launched, bringing together a range of left-wing and indigenous groupings. Its presidential candidate was Freddy Ehlers, a popular television presenter with a reputation for addressing controversial political issues. Pachacutec, founded in 1994, was an electoral organization which claimed to represent Ecuador's indigenous population. The alliance appeared new and attractive, and it

Abdalá Bucaram on stage, Guayaquil, October 1996   *AP*

seemed as if Ehlers might win enough votes to reach the second round of the elections.

But a bigger surprise was yet to come, when Abdalá Bucaram, the veteran leader of the PRE, outpolled both Ehlers and Paz, qualifying for the second round with Nebot. Dubbed *el loco* ("the madman"), Bucaram won the votes of Ecuador's poor farmers and urban slum-dwellers with attacks on the rich and promises of subsidies and better services. Where Ehlers had failed with his intellectual style, Bucaram succeeded with unabashed populism. The Quito elite was appalled by the prospect of a Bucaram presidency; the poor of Guayaquil and other cities flocked to his election rallies, where he sang, danced, and told jokes. In policy terms, little separated Nebot and Bucaram, but socially they were miles apart. "Abdalá is not allowed into the private clubs frequented by Nebot," wrote one national analyst. In the second round on July 7, Bucaram beat Nebot by a margin of eight per cent.

The Lebanese

During the 1996 election campaign, one newspaper published a cartoon of Bucaram, Nebot, and Dahik with the caption: "which country are we living in?" All are the descendants of Lebanese migrants, a group which has come to occupy a prominent position in Ecuadorean society. Immigration from the Middle East started at the end of the nineteenth century when Turkey invaded Lebanon, driving poor Lebanese families in search of a better life throughout Latin America. Armed with commercial acumen, many began selling sought-after items such as silk and jewelry before moving into small-scale manufacturing. The main area controlled by the Lebanese community, however, is banking, and Guayaquil's financial sector is run by a handful of families. Traditionally shunned by the Spanish-descended elite, the Lebanese were culturally marginalized and barred from the social clubs of the wealthy. As a result, they formed their own club and have maintained tight links through marriage and business dealings. Of the approximately 75 leading Lebanese-descended families, most are based in or near to Guayaquil, although some have settled in Quito or Cuenca. Important names include Adum, Bucaram, Isais, and Nebot. The Bucarams are a formidable political dynasty: Abdalá's sister, Elsa, was mayor of Guayaquil before choosing "self-exile" in Panama after allegations of corruption; his uncle, Asaad, was also mayor of Guayaquil, a deputy and influential power-broker; his cousin, Averroes, was president of Congress; other close relatives are deputies and ministers.

Bucaram embarked on a brief and chaotic period in office by performing the kind of policy U-turn beloved of other Latin American leaders such as Peru's Alberto Fujimori. Having promised to help the poor, he announced he would do so through "iron financial discipline," pushing through a package of austerity measures which included price increases for electricity and public transportation which outraged his supporters.

At the same time he seemed to go out of his way to alienate all sections of Ecuadorean society. He attacked the press, mocked the opposition parties, and caused a public scandal by inviting Lorena Bobbitt (the US-based Ecuadorean who achieved notoriety for severing her husband's penis with a kitchen knife) for lunch at the presidential palace.

He even annoyed nationalists by urging Peru and Ecuador to forgive and forget the dispute over the border which had led to war in 1995. Amid rumors of corruption scandals involving the extended Bucaram family, "The Madman's" popularity slid in spectacular fashion. By early 1997 only one per cent of Ecuadoreans approved of his performance. By early February, the country was paralyzed by a general strike, backed by business as well as labor, and Congress voted to fire Bucaram on the grounds of "mental incapacity." When the army decided to remove its support for Bucaram, he was doomed. After a period of confusion, during which Ecuador apparently had three rival presidents, the speaker of Congress, Fabián Alarcón, took over as interim president, pending elections in early 1998. Bucaram left the presidency and fled to Panama, muttering about returning to lead an armed revolt. However, it seemed unlikely that Ecuador's deepening political instability was over.

2 PEOPLE AND SOCIETY: THE ECUADOREANS

Modern Cowboys

About half of Ecuador's eleven million people are the descendants of Indians and Spaniards, known as *mestizos*. They mostly live in the towns, but many are also to be found in the small villages of the Andean mountains, where they are usually called *chagras*. The chagra is in many ways the modern-day Ecuadorean equivalent of the American cowboy. In former times they were the trustees of the hacienda owners and played a role as mediators between the *huasipungos* (peasant serfs) and the landlords.

Today chagras herd their cattle on the *páramo*, the high-lying grasslands on the mountain slopes of the Andes. Wrapped in their long ponchos, with their hairy rough-leather leggings and wearing *sombreros*, they are a distinctive sight on their small but speedy horses. No less distinct are the chagra women, the *chagrahuarmis*, straddling their horses in their traditional cos-

Chagras in Cañar region   *Leo van der Noort/HH*

tume. On feast-days young chagras enter the bull-ring where they take on wild bulls and steers with their bare hands. These tough *machos* are the living symbol of mestizo culture, and as Raúl Guarderas, the actor of chagra descent, says: "The most important features of a chagra are his love of the soil and his skill as cowboy and farmer."

Afro-Ecuadoreans

Black Ecuadoreans make up a significant part of the population in the country's coastal region. They are descended from the slaves who from the beginning of the eighteenth century were set to work in the plantations of the tropical lowland plain. Others worked in gold-mining or were used by the Spaniards as domestic servants. In the days of heavy physical work on the plantations the labor of one black slave was reckoned as equal to that of between four and eight Indians.

Although the slave trade was officially prohibited in 1821 it took until 1852 before slavery itself was abolished, but even then freedom proved elusive. The majority of the black population were still bound to their former owners by means of a system of debt tenancy, and not until 1881 was this system also abolished, meaning that the slaves could at last leave the plantations.

Today Ecuador's black population is estimated at just under one million, about ten per cent of the total population. Their social status is generally low, with most still working on banana plantations or in other types of agriculture, nowadays as poorly paid laborers. Those who try to escape rural poverty by migrating to town usually finish up in the building industry or find work as night-watchmen, messengers or caretakers. On the whole, Afro-Ecuadoreans suffer from poor education and very few reach higher positions in society. Anti-black racism tends to be common among all strata of society, and most Ecuadoreans are quick to denigrate the people they condescendingly call *negritos*. As the sociologist Fernando Carrión comments: "Every mestizo and Indian, no matter how poor and marginalized, declares himself to be an enemy of the black. This may be a kind of insecurity which he feels as a result of the pressure put on him by the social classes above him."

Afro-Ecuadoreans   *Tony Morrison/South American Pictures*

After the abolition of slavery most blacks continued to live in the coastal provinces of Esmeraldas and Manabí. A small community lives in the tropical Chota valley, in the Sierra north of Ibarra, where previously they worked on the sugar-cane plantations. They have retained their own culture which is most strongly expressed in music, dance and religious beliefs. Significantly, they and other black communities have practically never intermarried with mestizos or Indians.

Sierra Indians

About a quarter of all Ecuadoreans belong to one of eleven different indigenous peoples. Disease, violence, and expulsion from their lands

Otavalo market

Tony Morrison/South American Pictures

have been the main factors in the decline of a number of these peoples, including Amazon Indians such as the Huaorani, Siona-Secoya, and Cofán, so that in some cases communities can now be counted only in hundreds. Furthermore, various groups, including the Shuar and Ashuar, are now dispersed as a result of the border conflict with Peru which brought fighting to their traditional lands. Yet despite a range of pressures, different indigenous groups in the Andes, on the coast, and in the Amazonian rainforest have, to a greater or lesser extent, managed not just to survive but also to preserve their cultural identity.

The crowded markets in the Sierra are a spectacular kaleidoscope of colors, with indigenous fabrics creating a rainbow effect of deep red, cobalt blue, light green and a characteristic fuchsia purple. Indigenous clothing differs in the Andes from region to region but almost invariably stands out in sharp contrast to the monotonous yellow-green of the surrounding mountain slopes. In the north, for instance, live the Otavaleños, a community where women wear blue skirts and embroidered blouses and men sport long ponytails. The Saraguros from the south are conspicuous by their black clothes; tradition has it that they have worn mourning clothes ever since the death of Atahualpa. The Cañari women in the cold mountains of Azuay wear a black woolen cape, a thick woolen skirt, long knitted stockings, and a flat white hat with white or black ribbon. The Indians of Chimborazo and Tungurahua have a small black or brown hat and the women wear finely-pleated skirts.

The Otavaleños: Ecuador's Traveling Salesmen

Groups of pipe-playing Indian musicians, their hair traditionally tied in a ponytail, are a common sight in the streets and shopping centers of almost every European city. Some are from Bolivia or Peru, but in many cases they have come from Otavalo, a region to the north of Quito. At the beginning of summer Otavaleños cross over to European or other destinations to earn their bread as musicians and to sell their wares, usually handmade crafts – wall-hangings, pan-pipes, blouses, woven bags, alpaca jerseys – which come from practically every part of Ecuador, Peru, and Bolivia.

And within Ecuador itself the Otavaleños have a reputation as itinerant traders. The country's biggest Indian market, Otavalo, is a colorful collection of styles and products from all over the country. The Salasacas from the vicinity of Baños do their spinning and weaving almost entirely on behalf of the Otavaleños, and in every market in the country there are always a few Otavaleños to be found alongside the local Indians selling their fruit, vegetables, and livestock. As shrewd traders they are sensitive to trends in fashion and changing consumer tastes. In recent years traditional *ikat* patterns have been gradually giving way to recognizably more modern tapestry materials which are more in demand. Stylized bird and fish motifs are also conquering the markets, displacing traditionally symmetrical Andean patterns on wall-hangings.

The colorful diversity in the Sierra is a remnant from the colonial era when the Spanish hacienda owners forced the Indians on their land to wear a specific costume in order to tell the Indians from neighboring haciendas apart. In fact, all these Sierra groups belong to the Interandina Quichuas, who, with their approximately 1.5 million people, form the largest Indian grouping in the country. The common language, the Quichua introduced by the Incas, is the same from north to south and is closely related to the Quechua spoken in Bolivia and Peru.

Rainforest Indians

The largest groups of Indians in the Oriente are the 60,000 Quichuas in the provinces of Napo and Pastaza (in the vicinity of Puyo) and the 40,000 Shuar in the province of Morona Santiago. Although the Amazonian Quichuas speak the same language as the Quichuas in the Sierra, their culture and way of life are very different. Together with hunting, fishing, and wood

Waorani hunters   *John Man/South American Pictures*

gathering, they practice a form of itinerant farming, in which every few years they clear a few acres of jungle to make a new field or *chacra*. The old field is left fallow and the jungle is allowed to grow back. Although the individual chacra, on which corn, rice and cassava are cultivated, is still important, monoculture of palm and fruit trees is on the increase and cattle farming is also spreading through the region. As a result, traditional Quichua and Shuar lifestyles are changing very quickly. Their type of shifting agriculture requires large areas of land in order to give the jungle the chance of recovering, but because of increasing immigration of colonists from the Sierra available land is disappearing at an alarming rate. The advent of the oil industry in the Oriente is also affecting their way of life.

The number of Indians on the coastal plain is relatively small. Three ethnic groups dominate; in the north live approximately 4,000 Awas and in the center around Santo Domingo some 2,000 Tsachilas. The Tsachilas are famous for their *shamans*, the traditional medicine men. In the south, between Guayaquil and Machala, live some 7,000 Chacis. Just as in the Amazon region, the culture of the coastal Indians is under threat from the influx of Indian and mestizo migrants from the Sierra and from Colombia, who are attracted by job opportunities on the vast banana, coffee, and palm-nut plantations.

In 1986, in close collaboration with Colombia, where likewise about 10,000 Awas live, a "reservation" was established in the north in order to protect the Awas' own culture and way of life. Within this territory of approximately 400 square miles, the Awas have preferential rights to land and natural resources and are responsible for the preservation and management of the tropical rainforest. In an attempt to arrest environmental degradation they are experimenting with a sustainable combination of agriculture and forestry, producing fruit and vegetables as a way of decreasing dependence on timber which is becoming more and more scarce.

Racism

Al lomo del Indio, "on the Indian's back." This was the term used to describe the way in which whites and mestizos used to travel when making the descent down the Andes from Quito towards the Oriente. Indians were literally used as "people carriers," illustrating their utterly subordinated position in Ecuadorean society, rivaled only by the black population who are one step further down the social hierarchy. Since the beginning of the twentieth century this humiliating form of transport has not been used, but in many other respects little has changed in the burdens carried by indigenous people.

Racism has deep roots, and whites and mestizos continue to look on Indians as second-class citizens. In some districts, particularly in Cañar, this has resulted in violent confrontations between Indians and mestizos, especially the security forces, as in July 1994 when indigenous groups demonstrated against the new land reform law promulgated by the government. María Juana Chuma, Cañari and eyewitness of the battle which took place, gives the following account:

> After the bus had got stuck in the roadblock I ran back home through the mountains. Suddenly I saw thick clouds of smoke rising. It turned out that the headquarters of our organization in Cañar had been set on fire by mestizos and that there was heavy fighting between Indians and mestizos. Stones and bullets were flying around. Six people died and the whole building was destroyed. Very little is known of this in Quito and the government does nothing.

Poverty

Ecuador is one of the poorer countries of the South American continent. Per capita gross domestic product (GDP) in 1993 amounted to $1,170 ($1,490 in Peru, $1,400 in Colombia, and $710 in Bolivia). Like in Bolivia and Peru, wealth is distributed very unevenly and very much along ethnic lines, with the indigenous and black population bearing a disproportionately large share of poverty. Since most indigenous and blacks live in rural areas, this is where Ecuador's poverty is concentrated. While recent statistics show that more than 80 per cent of the population live in poverty and that many survive on the minimum wage of $160 per month, the wealthier middle classes are able to go shopping in Miami.

Rural women bear the brunt of poverty and are usually responsible for growing food, gathering wood for fuel, and looking after children. Their men often try to escape their grim predicament by seeking solace in drink, and in rural areas alcoholism is a widespread problem. When men go off to the town to seek work, they frequently spend their wages in such a way that nothing is left to send back to their family at home.

Domestic Violence

Women whose husbands have left home, either permanently or temporarily, are often left behind with a large number of children and have to try to make ends meet. But at least they do not have to put up with their husband's violence, since in Ecuador violence against women is a common phenomenon. In a macho culture, men often return drunk from the *cantinas* or local bars and can always find a pretext to beat their wives. In many cases, abuse of this sort is seemingly tolerated, even by its victims. As Flora, an Indian woman quoted in a study by Marjan Rens, says: "My husband always beat me when he was drunk and in those moments I was treated very roughly. [...] He beat me, I know, but I respected him anyway." In the towns, too, women face abuse and although this takes place less publicly in wealthier districts than in the poor *barrios*, domestic violence occurs in all strata of society. Machismo reinforces such violence and plays a large part in a society which tends to condone it and among the police who ignore it.

Yet women do not always suffer the violence passively. Several possibilities are open to them to escape abuse, among which are the traditional *padrinos de matrimonio*, godparents of a sort whom a young couple about to get married ask to watch over their marriage. Neighbors and (girl) friends might also be able to offer some mediation in marriage problems. Sometimes women take collective action, as in the case of Juana in the village of San Ignacio:

> There was once a man living up there with two women. He treated the one very badly and lived with the other, beating her, insulting her and doing all the things he ought not to do. And the poor woman had no family to help her. So then we women of the village got organized, we seized him and threw him in the water. After all, the same might happen to us, mightn't it?

After this incident, the women of the village decided to set up their own organization in order to prevent future violence. Quito, meanwhile, offers its women the possibility of refuge in a sort of sanctuary house.

Surviving in the City

Ecuador's cities offer some of the clearest symptoms of how poverty has spread in recent years. Thousands of small stalls selling all manner of goods have sprung up in the streets of Quito's colonial center. This phenomenon is a source of irritation to the government, which is trying to limit so-called "informal sector" activities, but without success. Unemployment fluctuates around the 50 per cent mark, and the economic liberalization policies of the 1980s and 1990s have eroded the purchasing power of large sections of the population.

Streetseller, Quito   *Tony Morrison/South American Pictures*

More and more people, including many children, are forced to seek a livelihood on a small scale by selling goods or offering services. It has been estimated that over the last few years more than 500,000 children aged between ten and seventeen have joined the already large army of itinerant peddlers in the informal sector. In Quito an increasing number of boys and girls wander up and down the popular Amazonas tourist street, hoping to sell chewing gum, sweets, cigarettes, or flowers, or to earn something by cleaning shoes. Many girls end up in prostitution.

Non-governmental and religious organizations have started up various projects aimed at improving life for the street children. According to the Salesian Fathers who run hostels in Quito, Guayaquil and Esmeraldas, 8,000 street children have passed through their doors since 1980. The best-known street child project is the Programa del Muchacho Trabajador, the Working Child Project, supported among others by the Central Bank of Ecuador. Over the whole country more than 4,500 children are accommodated every day in special centres, where they can receive education, have a place to play and are given something to eat. The project leaders are also trying to have children's rights enshrined in national legislation and have organized various conferences with titles such as "Today it is our turn to speak," "Together for the same dream" and "If we change... everything changes." The wide publicity which these conferences have generated has had an impact on public opinion and official bodies, and because of growing public awareness, Ecuador was in 1990 the first Latin American country and the third country in the world to ratify the Convention of Children's Rights set out by the United Nations.

Healthcare

The gulf between rich and poor is reflected in the two systems of Ecuadorean healthcare. Two-thirds of doctors, specialists, and hospitals are concentrated in Quito and Guayaquil, where only a quarter of the total population lives. There is also a huge difference in quality between the state hospitals, which have to struggle with a serious lack of space, medicines, and staff, and the

One of the thousands of
varieties of butterflies in the
Yasuni National Park
(Mario Garcia)

The eastern side of Ecuador,
the Oriente, a part of the
Amazon Basin, is almost
totally covered with tropical
rainforest, containing a huge
variety of fora and fauna.
Ecuador has declared parts
of the forest to be protected
nature reserves, such as the
Cuyabeno Game Reserve.
(Ana Maria Varea)

Yellow, blue and red were
the colors of the rebels
against Spanish rule. The
colors were incorporated
into the flag of the
Federation of Gran Colombia
and after 1830 Ecuador
retained the flag. Yellow for
sunshine, corn, and wealth,
blue for rivers, sea, and air,
red for the blood of patriots
who fought for freedom and
justice.
*(Vlaggen Dokumentatie Centrum
Nederland)*

Forest clearing along the Coca-La Yoja road. Colonization, woodcutting, and oil extraction represent the three greatest threats to the Amazonian rain forest. The population of the Oriente has grown threefold in a short space of time as a result of increasing economic activity.
(Lucho Suarez)

Along the banks of the Napo river. Cleared sections of the forest are often used for extensive cattle farming.
(Lucho Suarez)

A Siona Indian. Since ancient times the Siona people has inhabited the region of the Cuyabeno Game Reserve. Many of the original inhabitants of the rainforest are now dedicated to its conservation.
(Mario Garcia)

The biggest threat to the Ecuadorean Amazonian forest is the oil industry and especially the irresponsible way in which extraction is carried out. The slogans with which the state-owned oil company Petroamazonas praises itself on huge hoardings in Lago Agrio – "We are working for the future, protecting nature" – are open to dispute. At the beginning of 1995 the Ecuadorean government made practically the whole of the Oriente region available for oil prospecting, even large sections of the nature parks.
(Ana Maria Varea)

Pipelines bring the oil from the oil fields to the economic centers of Ecuador and to the transfer depots on the coast. The beginning of the Trans-Ecuador Pipeline cuts the village of Shushufindi right down the middle.
(Ana Maria Varea)

Pipelines break regularly. In the event of such a *derrumbe* (literally: caving in) the oil which leaks out is set on fire. This oil leak is near Shushufindi.
(Ana Maria Varea)

The gas which escapes during oil extraction is burned off. This process releases all kinds of poisonous substances and millions of insects die in the flames.
(Ana Maria Varea)

Waste oil is collected in piscinas (literally: swimming pools). These are often no more than shallow pits from which a large amount of oil leaks away and from which toxic vapors rise continuously. When a piscina is full it is "cleaned" by digging out some of the oil. The remainder – by far the greater part – is covered with a layer of earth.
(Ana Maria Varea)

"Cleaning" a piscina is extremely dirty and unhealthy work. The poisonous oil vapors get into the body through the nose, mouth, and skin pores. Because much more money can be earned than in other unskilled jobs, there are always plenty of candidates willing to do the dirty work.
(Ana Maria Varea)

private hospitals which are among the best in Latin America. Although such statistics do not inspire much optimism, the general state of the population's health has nevertheless shown an improvement since 1960: infant mortality has been halved and life expectancy has gone up by ten years to an average of 65.5 years.

The diseases which typically take a huge toll in many developing countries, such as diphtheria, dengue, yellow fever, and cholera, are no longer the main causes of death. In Ecuador too many people today die of diseases of the affluent society, the main causes of death being heart and vascular diseases, followed by intestinal infections and lung disorders. A further significant cause of death is traffic accidents.

Women normally make up a majority of hospital patients, many admissions being related to pregnancy and natal problems. Although abortion is officially banned, it is estimated that twelve per cent of admissions to gynecological departments are for the purpose of terminating a pregnancy.

Healthcare in Ecuador still leaves much room for improvement, but that has not prevented various governments from reducing its percentage of the state budget almost every year since the 1980s. Between 1992 and 1993 the allocation dropped from 6.4 per cent to 4.3 per cent, or less than $8 per head of the population.

Traditional Medicine

In the event of illness or other problems, a large number of Ecuadoreans, including those living in the cities, visit a shaman as well as the "official" doctor. Using all sorts of remedies, including an arsenal of herbs, colored dolls, amulets, eggs, guinea-pigs, and incantations, the shaman exorcises diseases such as *mal aire*, bad air or malaria, and *susto* or fright, and cleanses the body. Shamanism is a mixture of science, religion, and politics, and shamans, for whom all indigenous communities in the Sierra, Costa or Oriente have their own names, can cure disease, exorcise evil, settle disputes, and exercise ecological control.

The knowledge necessary to become a shaman is passed on from father to son or from mother to daughter and a complex ritual has to be undergone as part of this process with sacred animals such as the boa constrictor, the jaguar, the anaconda, the spider and the eagle having an important part to play. Elias Santi, one of the most famous shamans from the Amazon region, over 80 years of age, gives this account:

One day I went hunting, went a long way into the forest, and during the night was startled by a noise. I asked myself what it could be and went to look. Close by rapids in the river I saw two boas hanging down from a tree, fighting each other. I knew that to become a real shaman I had to overcome something dreadful and there now presented itself the opportunity of demonstrating my courage and defying one of the sacred animals. I therefore took hold of one of the boas, which looked round immediately, retracted its head and spat out a bright blue stone. I realized that this was a sign, I picked the stone up and swallowed it.

The shamans' reputation as healers is largely based on their knowledge of medicinal herbs; in Ecuador alone some 900 plants are used for medicinal purposes, including *uñas de gato* (cat's claw) and *sangre de dragó* (dragon's blood). This knowledge, however, is rapidly dying out and even the areas where the plants grow are shrinking under environmental pressure.

One way of preserving and developing this knowledge is by exporting genetic material from the jungle to foreign laboratories. Various pharmaceutical companies from North America are currently sending botanical experts to the Amazon region where they persuade indigenous shamans to teach them which plants can be used for which diseases. In 1989 a company was even set up for this very purpose, calling itself Shaman Pharmaceuticals Inc. The scientists return from their expeditions with samples of tree bark, seeds, flowers, and roots, which are used in experiments in order to manufacture approved drugs from the raw materials or to synthesize the genetic material. Drugs obtained in this way are then patented in the U.S. and eventually may be exported for sale in Ecuador, but by then they are likely to be too expensive for most of the population. In Ecuador, as in other Latin American countries, there is currently a lively debate under way as to how such knowledge transfer – or should it be knowledge theft? – can be regulated. The biggest problem is the lack of funds and technology necessary to develop a pharmaceutical industry in Ecuador itself from indigenous knowledge.

Quinine Comes from Ecuador

Theft of genetic material is nothing new. Around 1630 an Indian in Loja discovered that sap from the *quina* tree had a beneficial effect on people suffering from malaria. Powder from quina bark, which the Indians called fever powder, was then taken by the Jesuits to Spain where it was applied with success. By 1742, 23 varieties of quina were being classified in European botany texts. A lucrative trade in quina followed, which was to prove disastrous for the wooded slopes of Loja. Demand for the ingredient was so great that unscrupulous traders mixed the powder from the bark with other bark varieties, greatly damaging the reputation of Ecuadorean quinine. Even the discovery in 1820 of the active constituents of quina bark – quinine and cichonina – failed to stop the relentless disappearance of Loja's quina forests.

In 1860 the British government sent its representative Robert Cross and the biologist Richard Spruce to Loja where they collected seeds and cuttings from the red quina tree to ship to India. The British were not deterred by the export ban which the Ecuadorean government belatedly imposed the following year, since they had now come to realize that quinine was essential for keeping British troops in India healthy. After a few unsuccessful attempts the quina trees began to flourish on Indian plantations and by 1885 the world quinine market was dominated by Britain, Germany, and the Netherlands. Not only did this spell the end of quina cultivation in Ecuador, but it also meant that for a long time Asia was wrongly thought to be the birthplace of quinine.

Changing Tastes

Any official visitor is liable to be welcomed into an Andean village with a communal meal. If the village has acquired a certain degree of prosperity, the meal will probably consist of macaroni or spaghetti with tomato sauce. Indian families who have some disposable income have largely forsaken their traditional diets and are starting to buy "modern" foods such as pasta, sweets and western drink, all products with low nutritional value. This is a far-reaching change in their diet, particularly since in the Andes a number of traditional foods can be found with such high nutritional value that they are used today in space travel technology. These include, for instance, amaranto and quinoa, two cereals similar to millet which are rich in high-quality protein. Although the Incas regarded quinoa as sacred food, it is hardly cultivated any more and can only be bought now at a few Indian markets in the Sierra. The more than two hundred varieties of potato which grew in the Andes contributed traditionally to providing variety in local cooking. Potatoes still form an important ingredient in food and are popular cooked in the form of *llapingachos* or potato cakes with cheese. Yet over the last decades the number of varieties has been drastically reduced and Ecuadoreans are increasingly eating imported potatoes.

Education

In theory, each child in Ecuador is entitled to nine years of compulsory education, but figures reveal that most children attend school on average for only six years. In the countryside the drop-out rate in primary education is high and only a few go on to secondary education, largely because the population is very dispersed and the small number of schools and the cost of travel mean that schools are not easily accessible. Many poor peasant families also find the costs of registration, uniforms, and reading material prohibitive. Lack of resources also means that in many schools in the Sierra there is only one teacher to look after all six classes at the same time.

Rapid population growth and high illiteracy rates, particularly in rural areas, prompted governments to give more attention to education from about the mid-1960s onwards. Literacy campaigns were introduced for adults and

Reading in Quechua, Pimbaro

Julio Etchart/Reportage

bilingual education for Indian communities. While many new primary and secondary schools were built, the training of teachers did not keep pace and, particularly in secondary education, the number of pupils per teacher increased dramatically.

Over the last few years the growth in the number of school pupils has stagnated, a consequence of government cutbacks in spending and rising poverty. Although the 1989 constitution provides for allocating 30 per cent of government income to education, that percentage is never reached and in 1994 education only accounted for eighteen per cent of the budget.

Yet the result of earlier government policy was that illiteracy dropped from 44 per cent in 1950 to approximately fourteen per cent now. In urban districts and among men the percentage is even lower, but in those provinces which have a sizeable Indian population, such as Chimborazo, Cotopaxi, Bolívar, and Cañar, the figure is twice as high. There is a dearth of trained bilingual teachers, and Quichua – the first language of by far the greater number of Indians – is still not taught as a language in its own right.

A common complaint is that the quality of primary and secondary school education leaves much to be desired. One central problem is that investment in teacher training is woefully inadequate (amounting in 1993 to an average of only 60 cents or 40p per teacher in the primary school sector). As Father Espinoza, the headmaster of a secondary school in Quito, says:

"People often choose to become teachers only because there is usually nothing else for them to do." Teachers' salaries, meanwhile, are so low that there are regular and lengthy strikes to try and keep pace with rising living costs. There is a sharp contrast between state schools and the qualitatively much better private education, but private education is the preserve of only about twenty per cent of all pupils. Continuing government underfunding has also brought about a serious crisis in higher education.

Churches and Sects

In the night of November 24 and 25, a long procession of people winds its way up from the Quito valley, lighting up the road with torches or pocket-lamps, bound for Quinche where the Virgin of Quinche is venerated. An old man tells the story of the miraculous healing of his wife who had already been given up for dead by a dozen doctors. In order to thank the Virgin of Quinche, every year he undertakes the journey of some fifteen miles with tens of thousands of others. Quinche is only one of the many pilgrim shrines to which hundreds of thousands of pilgrims travel each year in order to pray for the healing of a sick person or to give thanks for a miraculous cure. These pilgrimages are an integral part of Roman Catholicism in Ecuador.

In colonial times Simón Bolívar described Ecuador as "a monastery," such was the power of the Church. Today, 96 per cent of Ecuadoreans are Roman Catholic and the Church's influence remains formidable. In 1994 the Archbishop of Quito successfully mediated between the government and Indian organizations in the conflict over the land reform law, and in the same year the bishops used their weight to have the *Ley Religiosa*, the Religious Education Act, passed, making religious education compulsory in state primary and secondary schools. Even national protest campaigns and student riots in which several people were killed, could not shift the Church from its position.

The number of Roman Catholics is decreasing in favor of religious sects originating in the U.S., including Seventh-Day Adventists, Jehovah's Witnesses and Pentecostalists. The influence of these groups has spread considerably since the mid-1960s, particularly in rural districts, where they work to win the allegiance of Indian *comunidades* or villages by means of small-scale development projects such as the building of latrines, setting up of market gardens, and construction of clinics. In the southern Sierra and the province of Chimborazo in particular, they are very active and their activities regularly lead to divisions among communities. In some areas, for instance, Indians speak of "those who drink" and "those who do not drink," a reference to the strict alcohol ban which the sects impose on their members.

Indigenous Renaissance

In the 1960s the inequitable distribution of land led to a wave of social unrest across Ecuador and the struggle for land reforms resulted in the founding of a number of smallholder organizations, such as FENOC, the National Federation of Farmers' Organizations, which counted among its members both mestizo and Indian farmers. Indigenous self-awareness was growing in the 1970s and in 1972 the first Indian organization, ECUARUNARI, was established, to be followed by many others since. The recognition of the right to vote of the illiterate, meaning that the countryside with its high proportion of illiteracy achieved political significance, was also an important factor in growing indigenous mobilization.

The interests of indigenous communities in different regions vary widely: both in the coastal region and in the Sierra the main issue is the struggle for land, while in the Amazon what is uppermost is resistance to colonization policies and the oil industry. For a long time the idea of a national Indian organization seemed utopian, and not until 1986 was the Confederación de Nacionalidades Indígenas del Ecuador (CONAIE, Confederation of Indigenous Nationalities of Ecuador) established, to which 26 regional organizations are affiliated and which, according to its own statements, represents Ecuador's approximately four million Indians.

It was in June 1990 that the CONAIE first came into its own during the *levantamiento indígena*, the Indian uprising. The Borja government had at the beginning of that year given foreign oil companies concessions to drill for oil in seven new concessionary areas, covering a total of 3.5 million acres. The Huaorani, whose territory is situated precisely in one of the concessionary regions, were furious and revolted, an uprising backed and broadened by a wide range of indigenous and non-governmental organizations.

The tactics used by the CONAIE, such as blocking the Panamericana, the country's most important north-south highway, and blockading food supplies to the big towns proved highly effective. The success of the levantamiento further strengthened indigenous self-confidence and ensured that demands for greater self-government and economic and human rights have since been taken seriously by governments. The 1994 mobilization against Sixto Durán Ballén's Agrarian Development Law, intended to "modernize" agricultural production by selling off communal indigenous lands, resulted in major concessions from the government. CONAIE leaders such as Luís Macas and Nina Pacari have become nationally recognized figures, and Macas was elected to Congress on the indigenous Pachacutec ticket in the March 1996 elections. Yet despite a much higher profile for indigenous issues and some very valuable propaganda victories against foreign oil companies such as Texaco, the concrete results achieved are so far limited. Dis-

Landless peasants plan occupation of idle land   *Julio Etchart/Reportage*

cussions between government and the CONAIE have yet to lead to real improvements for indigenous communities, and simmering conflict over land and other disputes has resulted in the Panamericana being regularly blocked since 1990.

Cochasquí: Reinforcing Indian Identity

A few miles north of Quito is the Cochasquí Archaeological Complex, consisting of fifteen pyramids covered with earth and a large number of dome-shaped burial tombs dating from the pre-Inca period. The exact function of the complex is difficult to reconstruct, and at present there are three theories which explain it as a religious site where astronomical observations were made, a fort on account of its strategic location, or a residence for the culture's rulers. For the Indians in the nearby village these theories are less important than their pride in a history transmitted by oral tradition; as one inhabitant puts it: "We want to reawaken our history and our traditions so that we shall come to know who we were." Supported by scientific research commissioned by the province of Pichincha, local people provide enthusiastic guided tours. They recount the tragic events which took place during the battles between Incas and Quitucaras on the very sites where they now live. The worst tale they have to tell is of the subterfuge which Huyana Cápac used to persuade Quiloga, the chieftainess commanding the Quitucaras, to come to his camp to make peace. When the woman warrior entered her enemy's tent, she fell into a deep pit onto projecting spears, dying a horrible death. Not surprisingly, this event broke the morale of her troops and her 30,000-strong army of Quitucaras was subsequently hacked to pieces. The name of the Laguna de Yaguarcocha (the Lake of Blood), close to Ibarra, is a reminder of this massacre.

One of the high points during the guided tour is the pre-Colombian herb garden. In order to prevent knowledge of the medicinal qualities of herbs becoming lost, the curators of Cochasquí devote a great deal of time to collecting and cultivating various kinds of herbs. In addition to its function as a tourist attraction and educational center, the site also has a symbolic function. Every year in June the *Inti-Raymi* festival is celebrated here, the festival of the solstice, to which indigenous people come from far and wide.

Non-Governmental Organizations and the Environment

The gap between indigenous or peasant organizations on the one hand and government bodies on the other is seemingly insurmountable. Quito's bureaucracy inhabits a different world from that of isolated rural communities, and there is little communication between them. All too often government bodies initiate programs and policies which are totally opposed to the needs and wishes of indigenous and *campesino* communities. In order to bridge this gap between community-based groups and government agencies a large number of non-governmental organizations (NGOs) were set up in the 1970s and 1980s. In the Oriente alone there were 28 such organizations active in the mid-1990s, most of them working closely with a particular target group: Indians, *colonos* (colonists), women, street children, and other social sectors. Many NGOs receive money from abroad, primarily from Europe and North America, while a few, such as the Fondo Ecuatoriano Populorum Progressio (FEPP) are financed by the Church.

From the mid-1970s onwards it was becoming increasingly clear that Ecuador was facing serious environmental problems, and this gave birth to various NGOs which dealt specifically with ecological issues. Because since then the funding available for environmental projects has increased dramatically, other organizations already in existence have likewise begun to address the environment. By 1993 there were already 61 officially registered "green" NGOs in Ecuador, some such as Fundación Natura, specializing in environmental education in schools, others like Ecociencia, primarily concerned with research or with the legal dimensions of environmental control. Despite the growth in environmentalism, there is little coordination between the various NGOs and even a good deal of rivalry. In 1994 the environmental organization, Arco Iris, was awarded a prize from the United Nations in recognition of its efforts to conserve a threatened forest in the province of Loja.

The state, too, has recently been showing greater interest in environmental control and to this end the Comisión Asesor Ambiental de la Presidencia de la República de Ecuador (CAAM), a kind of ministry for environmental affairs, was set up in 1994, with among other tasks, the aim of formulating a national policy plan for the environment. What is important is that the CAAM has more powers of decision-making and greater resources than previous environmental departments. It is, however, too early to be able to predict whether these efforts will have any effect and whether the policy produced will in fact eventually be implemented.

3   ECONOMY AND ENVIRONMENT: FRAGILE FRONTIERS

Oil money has changed the face of Ecuador out of all recognition in the brief space of 30 years. Since the early 1970s the country has been transformed from an agricultural economy into one in which the services sector, mining, and, to a lesser extent, industry now play an important role. The rapid development of the oil industry has, however, made the country highly dependent on a single export product; today Ecuador's economy is driven by the price of oil on the world market.

During the 1970s when oil prices were buoyant and loans were cheap, GDP showed avarage annual growth of as much as 9.5 per cent. But in the 1980s, when prices fell and the debt crisis emerged, growth shrank to an average of just over two per cent. In 1990 Ecuador again experienced a short-lived boom when oil prices rose in response to the Gulf War, but growth soon dropped back to an average of three per cent in the period 1993-6. Overall, between 1980 and 1992 per capita GDP annually fell by 0.3 per cent.

Import Substitution and Debt

In order to stimulate industrial development the government decided in the 1960s and 1970s, like other regional governments, to adopt what were termed import substitution policies. A central plank in this economic strategy is a system of high import taxes and other disincentives, with the aim of making domestic manufacturing viable by discouraging cheap imports. Implementation of this policy does, however, entail high levels of domestic investment in the setting up of industry and the import of "capital goods" (machinery and suchlike) in order to start up production. In the 1960s and 1970s some of the oil money was used to establish state-owned industrial companies or to purchase shares in existing companies. It soon became apparent that Ecuador's own capital was insufficient but with the oil reserves as a guarantee there was no problem in borrowing extra funds abroad.

The policy of import substitution did not result in the development of the dynamic industrial sector that had been predicted. Most of the dollars earned from oil sales and borrowed abroad were spent on consumption (including subsidies for essential consumer goods), on investment in trade, and on speculation. But the policy also had its supporters who claimed that in an economy protected by high tariff walls the government had greater scope for controlling economic and social policy. The government, they claimed, was able to ensure by means of subsidies that most Ecuadoreans' purchasing power was kept stable. Problems only began to pile up when the government could no longer earn enough to pay for this redistributive policy. After the 1981 debt crisis interest rates rose steeply and, at the same time, the price of oil and of Ecuador's agricultural exports plummeted. Like many other developing countries, Ecuador was forced to keep borrowing simply in order to meet interest and capital payments on earlier loans, with the result that the government slipped further into debt. This has meant that during the last ten years the country has had to ask the International Monetary Fund (IMF) for balance-of-payments support on a number of occasions. The conditions which the IMF has attached to its loans have included a drastic reduction in government spending in areas such as education and health. Subsidies have also been slashed on consumer goods such as gas, and thousands of state-sector jobs have been lost, with more than 20,000 government employees fired since 1993.

In spite of repeated debt rescheduling, allowing repayment to be spread over a longer period, Ecuador's debt stood at over $16 billion in mid-1996. In terms of the size of the economy, this means that Ecuador has the fourth highest debt in the world and that every inhabitant owes some $1,400 to the IMF, World Bank, and other financial institutions.

Liberalization and Privatization

Since President Febres Cordero (1984-8) the policy of import substitution has gradually been dropped in favor of free-market reform. Rodrigo Borja's social-democratic government marked time for a number of years, but Sixto Durán Ballén continued Febres Cordero's objective of liberalizing the economy. His government tried to make Ecuador attractive to foreign companies in search of cheap labor and generous tax concessions. Most important, however, was an extensive proposed program of privatization which was intended to reduce government spending by getting rid of loss-making state-owned companies. In total there are about 200 fully state-owned firms in Ecuador as well as a number of companies in which the government owns between twenty and thirty per cent of shares.

Sixto Durán Ballén's liberalization policy recorded few real successes, perhaps with the exception of the removal of Petroecuador's monopoly on petroleum distribution. Ecuador, due to its small domestic market, has never been really attractive to foreign investors and countries closer to the U.S., such as Mexico, can compete on labor costs and other incentives. Nor did the privatization program get off the ground; instead of seeing a projected 80 per cent of state companies pass into private hands, Sixto Durán Ballén's government presided over the transfer of a handful of public-sector concerns. Only the bankrupt national airline, Compañía Ecuatoriana de

48

Aviación, was sold off, along with some smaller state interests in hotels, restaurants and road-building. Opposition parties in Congress managed to hold up any large-scale privatization by blocking the necessary legislation, while public opinion polls revealed that eighty per cent of Ecuadoreans were against the program. The fear that vital sectors of the economy, such as telecommunications and electricity, might fall into foreign hands, is the underlying reason for overwhelming public opposition. According to Marcel Laniado, then director of the privatization agency, such fear is unfounded: "The intention is to privatize only those government concerns which do not fulfil any social function and in which the government has no interest, such as the cement industry."

Free-market reformers also face the powerful opposition of the Ecuadorean military, an economic as well as political force to be reckoned with. Between 1972 and 1979, when the army ruled the roost, petro-dollars flowed into the country and the generals did not hesitate to consolidate their interests with an eye to the future. As well as the defense industry the armed forces also own hotels, banks, and an airline company, for instance, and it was therefore no surprise that they were opposed to Sixto Durán Ballén's privatization plans. The conflict with Peru has considerably enhanced their prestige and increased support for their point of view. Whether any government will challenge such vested interests remains to be seen.

Yet the greatest problem facing Ecuador's economy is its structural imbalance. The country continues to earn its foreign currency almost exclusively from the exploitation of natural resources – oil and agricultural products – and industry is relatively insignificant. At the same time, the concentration of capital and wealth in the hands of the few is increasing rather than decreasing, while the economic well-being of the great majority of the population is in decline.

In 1995, 80 per cent of the population could be termed poor and 55 per cent could not provide for their basic food needs – a situation comparable to the 1940s before banana exports and subsequently the oil industry brought some degree of prosperity. The crippling burden of foreign debt, persistent budgetary deficits, the price volatility of Ecuador's exports, and chronically high levels of inflation and unemployment complete a grim picture of an economy in which more and more people can only just survive.

Oil: Production and Control

Pumping up oil in the coastal region of Santa Elena began in 1917 and the search for oil in the Amazon region took off in 1921 when the U.S. Standard Oil Company was given the first concession. It was not until 1967, however, that the first oil field, owned by Texaco Gulf, started up production near Lago Agrio. That moment marked the opening up of the Oriente, and in the

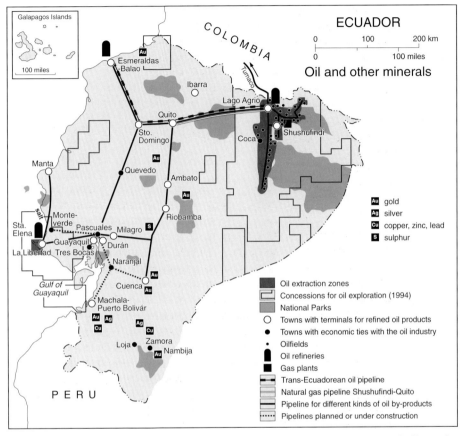

following years dozens of airstrips and 300 miles of roads were built. In the early years all prospecting and oil extraction was controlled by foreign companies. Standard Oil Company, Texaco, Gulf, Shell, Exxon, and Maxus each had their own oil fields and lent the name of their company to the little settlements which housed the oil workers, such as the village of Shell near Puyo. In 1971 the nationalist military government set up a state company, the Corporación Estatal Petrolera Ecuatoriana (CEPE, the Ecuadorean State Oil Corporation), and in 1989 the Borja government took over the last shares of the foreign companies in oil production and shortly afterwards the CEPE was restructured and given a new name: Petroecuador. Significantly, the government denied that the buy-out of Texaco's facilities amounted to nationalization and insisted that foreign investment remained necessary in terms of capital and technical know-how.

Oil production grew between 1972 and 1981 by an average of nine per cent each year, and this spectacular growth prompted the decision in 1973, the year of the first oil crisis and the price boom, to join OPEC. After 1980, however, the price of crude oil began to fall, slightly at first and then seriously after 1985, and in order to maintain export revenue and government income, production levels had to be stepped up vigorously. New oil fields were brought into production and between 1987 and 1991 output increased by a third.

Rising production led to conflict with OPEC which was trying to stabilize world oil prices by limiting its members' ouput. Having exceeded its quota on several occasions, Ecuador decided in 1992 to relinquish its membership of OPEC, intending to further boost production. The move resulted in an almost six per cent increase in export volume within a year, albeit at lower prices than anticipated. That year the government also unveiled plans to effectively double production to 575,000 barrels per day (bpd) by 1996, although 1997 levels, limited by inadequate pipelines and other infrastructure, are still nearer 390,000 bpd.

In the 1990s the contribution made to total export income by oil has stood at between 40 and 50 per cent, depending on world prices. The U.S. is the main market for Ecuadorean oil, accounting for approximately half of exports in 1995, followed by the Dutch Antilles. At the present rate of production and based on proven reserves, Ecuador's oil will be exhausted within about twenty years. The country does, however, have considerable reserves of natural gas which at the moment are under-exploited.

Faced with the prospects of dwindling reserves, recent governments have been eager to invite foreign oil companies to search for fresh fields. Since 1985 there have been several rounds of granting concessionary areas to interested companies to drill for oil, and with the 1993 investment law the Sixto Durán Ballén government considerably widened the scope for transnational involvement. During the 1994 round six concessions were granted to companies such as Triton, Oryx, Amoco-Mobil, City, and Tripetrol, while in 1996 a further auction awarded contracts to U.S.-based Atlantic Richfield and Argentina's Compañia de Gas y Combustibles. These latest issues have served to designate the whole of the Amazon region, including all Indian territories and national parks, as an oil extraction region. According to the constitution, the land belongs in principle to the people who live on it, but all the minerals under the ground belong to the state, which can make decisions regarding mining and drilling without consultation.

Oil and the Environment

Large areas of Ecuador's Oriente have been devastated by the oil industry, while successive governments have done little to prevent the ruin of what they see as a "frontier," to be exploited at will. A combination of deforestation and contamination has caused immense damage to huge swathes of the Amazon, and Petroecuador, the state corporation, is subject to little or no regulation.

The negative impact of oil extraction begins at once during the process of prospecting. An investigation in 1989 revealed that the U.S. company ARCO built 1,368 helicopter landing sites and carried out almost a thousand explosions in its search for oil, resulting in a devastation of more than 2,500 acres of jungle. Once oil pumping is under way, the consequences for the environment are even more drastic, as, for instance, large quantities of crude can leak from the *piscinas*, the pits in which waste oil is collected. Numerous heavy metals are found in the waste products, including cadmium, chromium, copper, lead, magnesium, mercury, nickel, and zinc, all of which leak into rivers and streams. The oil pipelines themselves leak constantly and occasionally even break altogether. During the twenty years of its existence the Trans-Ecuador Pipeline has broken 30 times, releasing a total of almost 400,000 barrels of oil into the Amazon basin, almost one and a half as much as during the Exxon Valdez disaster in Alaska.

In 1993 a $1.5 billion lawsuit was filed in New York against Texaco by indigenous and peasant groups, claiming that the U.S. transnational had been negligent in its Oriente operations. Texaco was publicly supported by the Ecuadorean government, which insisted that legal action of this sort would discourage further foreign investment. After four years, the lawsuit ran out of steam.

Manufacturing

During the 1970s the industrial sector expanded rapidly, averaging annual growth of 10.5 per cent and eventually accounting for nineteen per cent of GDP by 1980. Both the oil industry and the policy of import substitution ensured that new factories mushroomed around Quito and Guayaquil, with chemical, wood and paper, and metal-processing sectors the main beneficiaries of this expansion. But import substitution soon came to grief and between 1980 and 1992 industrial production grew by a mere 0.2 per cent. Foreign companies were reluctant to invest in Ecuador since the domestic market was too small, meaning that the industrial sector, compared with that of neighboring countries, was underdeveloped and overprotected. So far, figures show that regional economic cooperation within the Andean Pact trade bloc has had little effect on this situation and has opened the economy to cheaper imports from Colombia and Venezuela.

In export terms, industry is of secondary importance, contributing only about $200 million out of a total of $4-4.5 billion a year. The Durán Ballén government tried to attract export industries to Ecuador, promoting

Guayaquil and Esmeraldas as ideal places to establish low-wage *maquiladoras* or assembly factories. Foreign companies are exempt from various taxes and employment legislation has been relaxed to enable employers to take on part-time workers and dismiss employees easily. Since 1993 foreign companies have enjoyed the same rights as national companies, with the result that foreign investment actually doubled in 1993 after constantly falling between 1988 and 1992. Most foreign investment comes from the U.S. and is targeted at the food and drink manufacturing sector.

Three-quarters of all industries are located in Quito and Guayaquil. Traditional sectors such as food processing, beverages, textiles, and tobacco predominate, but the most interesting newcomer during the last few years has been the car assembly plant of General Motors-Suzuki. Most industrial workers are employed in small family businesses, and firms with more than 500 workers are rare in Ecuador.

Agriculture

Notwithstanding the spectacular rise of the oil industry, more than half of Ecuador's foreign currency earnings comes from agriculture and fishing. The importance of this sector in employment terms, however, has fallen sharply, with only 30 per cent of the workforce employed in farming or fishing in 1990 as opposed to more than 60 per cent in 1969. The contribution of agriculture to GDP has followed a similar trend, falling from 24 per cent in 1970 to twelve per cent in 1995.

From a distance the slopes of the Andes look like multi-colored patchwork quilts. The colors of the small fields, sometimes clinging to the steepest of slopes, vary according to the season of the year and to what crops are growing on them. Above tree level nothing can be cultivated, and this is where the *páramos* lie, the grasslands which are often owned communally and which are principally used for grazing cattle.

The legacy of the *huasipungo* system has to a large extent determined patterns of land ownership in the Sierra. Although during the turn-of-the-century "Liberal Revolution" of Eloy Alfaro this system was considerably reformed, it was not completely abolished until 1964. From then, in theory at least, the ex-*huasipungueros* had a right to their own plot of land, but for many years little materialized in practice. Since most estate owners successfully managed to prevent the dividing up of the *haciendas* there was soon a huge shortage of land. Nevertheless between 1964 and 1984 a total of 1.8 million acres of agricultural land was shared out among 95,000 families, each of whom was given on average about seventeen acres. Many parcels of land have since been fragmented as a result of shared inheritance and many families today own less than twelve acres, not enough to live on.

Smallholdings in Latacunga area   *KIT Photobureau*

Land distribution remains extremely skewed; 1994 figures showed that 1.6 per cent of farms in the Sierra accounted for 43 per cent of land. As a result, many Indians and *mestizos*, particularly men, turn their backs on rural life and go to look for work in the city or in the Oriente. The women, however, mostly remain behind in order to work the land or look after the children.

Since 1964, then, a number of haciendas have been split up, but many *campesinos* still work as laborers on the lands of the *latifundistas* or estate owners. While the large landowners managed to keep the best holdings, the campesinos were often allocated small plots which soon became exhausted by over-cultivation. This is one reason why indigenous farmers are taking over land on ever steeper slopes and are opening up the páramo. Not only is there a risk of failed harvests as a result of sudden night-frost, but a very vulnerable ecological area is being irreparably damaged in the process. Large areas of the Sierra which were previously used as agricultural land have now been eroded to such an extent that they are now only suited for grazing small animals. Poverty and land hunger on the part of small farming communities hence pose the greatest threat to nature in the Andes.

Colonization and Deforestation in the Oriente

The Ecuadorean Amazon region covers 50,000 square miles of tropical rainforest, a little less than half the total surface area of the country. Twenty per cent of the Oriente has been designated as national parks or game reserves, meaning that officially no felling, hunting, or fishing is permitted. But this demarcation takes no account of the people already living in these regions, and various indigenous groups are dependent upon what the jungle offers, while the few park-rangers, who on average have to look after 74,000 acres each, make little difference.

In spite of the protection supposedly offered by the national parks, the Oriente is being deforested at a rapid rate, most of the damage caused not by the commercial exploitation of wood but by the *colonos*, the colonists who leave the barren Andes in search of land and a livelihood. This colonization is in part spontaneous and in part the result of government policy. Since the first land reform law in 1964 governments have tried to solve the problem of land shortage and unemployment in the Sierra by encouraging mass migration to the Oriente, where, it seemed, agricultural potential was unlimited. The authorities in Quito have also always believed that Peru would be less likely to seize an inhabited agricultural area than an expanse of uninhabited rainforest.

Government policy will grant ownership of a piece of land to any colono as soon as he can show that he is using it agriculturally, hence encouraging large-scale deforestation. Between 1964 and 1984, 5.7 million acres were shared out among some 52,000 families. When in the 1970s the oil companies began to move into the jungle and built roads, a further wave of migration followed in their wake. In all, almost 145,000 colonos settled in the Oriente in the 1970s and 1980s, forming more than one-third of the population by 1990.

In their new holdings the colonos tend to use their traditional, often Andean, farming methods. But if at first the permanantly green exterior of the Amazonian forest seems to promise fertile land, the thin soil layer is exhausted after a year or two and the land can then only be used as pasture on which an average of 2.5 acres provides grazing for fewer than two head of cattle.

The environmental consequences are catastrophic. Once the jungle has been used as pasture it cannot recover because the cattle trample down the clay soil so firmly that seeds – even grass seeds – can no longer germinate. During the last 30 years almost 230,000 acres a year have been lost to deforestation in the Amazon region, equal to one per cent of the total surface area of jungle. Despite various government programs and projects sponsored by international organizations, the area which is replanted every year represents only a fraction of what is lost. At the present rate of clearing it is estimated that the Oriente will have no jungle left by the year 2020.

The Banana Industry

The vast banana plantations in the coastal provinces of Guayas, El Oro and Los Ríos seem to stretch away into infinity, with only the blue plastic sacks wrapped round the bunches of bananas providing a change of colour in the monotonous green landscape. The luxurious homes which dot the plantation valleys suggest that there is money to be made from bananas, but the squalid settlements which house the laborers reveal another dimension of poverty.

Ecuador is the world's biggest exporter of bananas and the industry provides its second largest source of export revenue, earning $845 million in 1995. Most are grown on medium-sized plantations of 120 acres on average, but are traded by a handful of large transnational companies. Bananas are not only important as a source of income but are also vital in employment terms. Directly or indirectly, the livelihoods of two million Ecuadoreans depend on the industry, whether in cultivation, distribution, exporting, or informal roadside selling.

Ecuador's biggest banana company, Exportadora Bananera Noboa, is also its most powerful corporation, owning 90 per cent of arable land in Los Ríos province and having a turnover of more than $1.1 billion in 1995. The fifth largest banana company in the world, Noboa controls production and distribution and owns its own fleet for shipping bananas to overseas markets. Diversification into other export crops and banking has ensured that the company has been able to weather a number of crises, while its family shareholders and top executives have close links to conservative political parties.

Despite Noboa's strength, the influence of U.S. multinationals such as Del Monte and Standard Fruit is also significant. They buy their bananas through middlemen and dominate the most important markets – the U.S. and Europe. The 30 or so smaller companies which were active in the banana trade in the 1960s have had to give up their independence and are now all tied to one or another of the big foreign exporters. Within Ecuador itself, however, they have managed to preserve their power by investing in lucrative activities such as cattle ranching, cocoa production, and shrimp farming.

The European Union and Bananas

Nowadays it is easy to buy a bunch of *guineos*, the first-class export-quality bananas, from the hordes of hopeful vendors who wait by the traffic lights in Ecuador's cities. Before 1992 the best bananas were often in short supply, as most ended up in the supermarkets of Europe. But in April of that year change came when the European Union issued a directive setting a limit to

Bananas on sale, Saquisilí
Julio Etchart/PANOS Pictures

the importation of so-called "dollar bananas" from Latin America and stipulating that imports above this maximum level would attract a high rate of import duty. The quota system was designed to protect banana producers in the Africa-Caribbean-Pacific (ACP) countries (practically all of them former colonies of EU countries) and EU producers themselves in places like the Canary Islands, Madeira, Crete, and the French Overseas Departments. The EU was concerned that if the market was completely free, the lower-quality and more expensive bananas from these regions would be swept aside.

Poison and Perfection

According to the European Union, the ideal banana is 5.5 inches long and 1 inch thick, is not abnormally bent, has no brown spots and boasts a uniformly yellow peel. In order to obtain this "ideal" banana pesticides have to be used on a large scale. One of the most common and dangerous chemicals which goes into Ecuador's pesticides is *1-2 dibromo-3 chloropropano* (DBCP), which can cause infertility, spontaneous miscarriage, and congenital defects. Since it also pollutes air, water, and soil, its use has been banned in the U.S. since 1977. Not, however, in Ecuador, where a number of foreign companies use this product with no restriction whatsoever. Various trade union organizations have now got together and are collecting evidence to show the damage done by the chemical poison. This will inevitably lead to legal proceedings against a number of multi-national companies who continue to use DBCP.

Safety regulations which should be observed when using pesticides are widely ignored, and banana workers regularly show serious symptoms of poisoning. The pollution caused by banana cultivation also extends further than the plantations themselves. Some of the pesticides find their way to the sea via rivers where they become a threat to shrimp farms. The use of chemicals also means that small banana growers are at a disadvantage since many find intensive chemical treatments too expensive.

Since the EU policy came into place, Noboa and other exporters have tried to diversify export markets to non-EU European countries and Asia with considerable success. This has partly compensated for restrictions within the EU, but Ecuador has also joined the U.S., Honduras, Guatemala, and Mexico in a World Trade Organization panel to protest at Brussels' licensing system which, it claims, is contrary to the free-trade principles of the General Agreement on Trade and Tariffs (GATT), to which the EU is a signatory.

Cocoa and Coffee

Low prices on the world coffee market pushed down export income for seven consecutive years in the 1980s and 1990s, and for harvests of more or less equal volume Ecuador earned $299 million in 1986 but only $80 million in 1992. Not until 1993 was there any improvement in coffee exports ($101 million) and recovery continued in 1994 and 1995 as a result of frost damage to Brazilian coffee production.

Coffee is Ecuador's fourth most important export; about a fifth of all agricultural land is planted with the crop but the yield per acre is low – the lowest in Latin America – and the quality is indifferent. Years of falling prices have brought about a restructuring of coffee growing. The older plantations in the coastal province of Manabí are slowly being replaced by new plantations in the Andes and in the southern provinces of Loja and El Oro. Here, new varieties are being cultivated which are more resistant to disease and offer both better quality and higher yields.

The trend in cocoa cultivation is much the same. In 1950 this crop was still the country's most important export, but since then its importance has diminished and in recent years export income has been hit by wild price fluctuations. A combination of bad weather and low world-market prices reduced earnings from $138 million in 1985 to a mere $35 million in 1992 but figures recovered to $133 million by 1995. After the U.S. the Dutch chocolate industry is the most important customer for Ecuadorean cocoa.

Cut Flowers

Recent years have seen a rapid rise in cut flower exports, producing more than $25 million a year in the 1990s as opposed to a mere 0.5 million in the 1980s. Most flowers are flown straight to the U.S. but some are traded in European flower auctions, where roses are the most popular bloom, followed by the flower arranger's staple, gypsophila.

Most cut flowers are grown in the northern Andes near Otavalo and Cayambe, where the climate in the *hoyas* (valleys) between the two Andean mountain ranges of the Andes is ideally suited to flower-growing and where plastic hothouses provide sufficient protection against night frosts. Flower-growing also generates local employment: 15,000 workers, mainly women, are directly employed by the flower companies, while another 60,000 are estimated to earn an indirect living from the industry. As in neighboring Colombia, there are concerns over the environmental and health implications of massive pesticide use, and smallholders complain that the flower-growers monopolize scarce water supplies.

Vegetable Ivory

One export which has been gaining in importance during recent years is *tagua* or vegetable ivory. Ecuador is the only country in the world to export this product, which in 1991 raised $6.3 million. On the outside the tagua is an unsightly brown nut, and its inside consists of white compact fruit that is soft to the touch. It is almost impossible to imagine that processed tagua nut is indistinguishable from genuine ivory. After being harvested, the nut has to harden over a period of time, after which it can be cut and carved in any shape required. Processing tagua products is a fairly costly business, and expensive machines are required to work the hard nuts. In the province of Chimborazo there are some 27 small family businesses processing the nuts, and in Manta on the coast about a hundred. The most common tagua products are buttons, but it is now also possible to buy ornaments and chess sets. The ban on the export of elephant ivory has increased the importance of tagua, for 200 pounds of nuts will produce as many products as one elephant tusk with a value of ten thousand dollars.

Shrimps

When the shrimpboats return to the village of Palestina in the province of Guayas with their catch, dozens of young children rush out onto the beach and form groups of between ten and fifteen. Seated around a huge plastic sheet, they work at high speed to clean the shrimps (*camarones*) which the fishermen dump in their midst.

After China, Indonesia, and Thailand, Ecuador is the world's fourth largest shrimp exporter. Although compared to these countries its export volumes are low, earnings, particularly from the U.S. market, are significant, and during the last ten years shrimps have taken third place in export revenue after oil and bananas. For shrimps, too, prices tend to vary from year to year but the general tendency is upwards, and 1995 saw a record yield of $678 million.

Most shrimps are farmed in the Gulf of Guayaquil where foreign capital has fueled a huge expansion in the industry. But shrimp producers are increasingly at risk from the overuse of pesticides in banana cultivation, some of which finishes up in rivers and the sea, causing a variety of diseases such as "bull syndrome" which kills young shrimps. For this reason shrimp farmers are moving further and further north, and in recent years the biggest expansion has been in the province of Esmeraldas.

Threatened Mangrove Forests

Intensive shrimp-farming has also damaged the delicate ecological balance in the region, especially among the mangrove forests which used to cover much of the coastline. Mangroves provide a vital ecological function, offering essential shelter from the strong currents of the cold Humboldt Stream and predators to a wide variety of species. Surveys have shown that mangrove forests act as a habitat for up to 45 different species of bird, fifteen species of reptile, seventeen species of crustacean and hundreds of kinds of fish. Moreover, this ecologically vulnerable zone is vital to shrimp-farming itself, since mangrove forests also provide protected incubating chambers for young shrimps. Yet a number of national and foreign companies have already cleared large areas of mangrove in order to build shrimp-farming ponds, ignoring protests from local inhabitants who have traditionally depended on the wealth of crustaceans, and fish from these coastal waters. By 1993 shrimp farms covered an area of 320,000 acres, while mangrove forest had shrunk from 500,000 acres in 1969 to 400,000 acres by the early 1990s.

Tourism and Eco-tourism

The popular tourist area around the Avenida Amazonas in Quito literally teems with travel agents and tour guides, offering trips which vary from an economy mini-cruise in the Galápagos archipelago to luxury trips in a floating hotel in the Oriente. Ecuador certainly has no shortage of tourist attractions. Its natural scenery varies from high mountain ranges to lush rainforest; there are fine examples of Spanish colonial architecture; examples of indigenous culture are to be found almost everywhere. In spite of the border conflict with Peru, Ecuador is relatively stable, safe, and cheap for foreign visitors. Not surprisingly, in recent years the number of tourist arrivals has risen by fifteen per cent annually to 430,000 in 1992, when $192 million was earned through tourism, the fifth most important source of foreign currency.

Tourist and seals, the Galápagos

Hilary Bradt/South American Pictures

Conservation of the Galápagos

The Galápagos Islands are without doubt Ecuador's main tourist attraction; in 1993 some 42,000 visitors passed through the islands, while in the 1960s tourists were few and far between. The islands were officially "discovered" in 1535 and in 1570 they appeared for the first time on a map with the name Insulae de los Galápagos, islands of the giant tortoises. In the following centuries the archipelago became a favorite port of call for pirates, whalers and seal hunters who, as tradition has it, kept themselves alive by taking thousands of tortoises on board as fresh meat.

Ecuador annexed the archipelago in 1832, and from then on the first "permanent" inhabitants migrated to the island of Santa María. Most of these were criminals and prostitutes who had been banished from the mainland. The most famous nineteenth-century visitor was the scientist Charles Darwin, who arrived while undertaking a world voyage in 1845 on his ship *The Beagle*. In his account of the Galápagos, *The Voyage of the Beagle*, he reports his amazement at the region's ecological variety: "The natural history of this archipelago is very remarkable: it seems to be a little world within itself; the greater number of its inhabitants, both vegetable and animal, being found nowhere else."

The Galápagos were created by a series of volcanic eruptions and the islands are in fact the tops of volcanoes which rise up from the sea-bed. The oldest are some four to five million years old. With more than 2,000 volcanic craters and some 50 recorded eruptions since its discovery, the archipelago is one of the most active volcanic regions in the world. The volcanos are situated where two tectonic plates, the Nazca and the Cocos plates, are slowly drifting apart; volcanic activity is strongest in the northwest of the island group.

From a scientific point of view, the Galápagos are a unique region because the islands have never been connected to the mainland but have always been separated by six hundred miles of ocean. All indigenous plants and animals must have reached the islands by air, or by swimming or floating on pieces of wood. The original fauna comprises seabirds, reptiles, sea mammals, a few small land mammals, and relatively few insects, almost all of which are only found here and frequently only on one of the islands. It was specifically the characteristics of the fauna, in particular the finches, which put Darwin on the trail of the theory of evolution.

The ecology of the islands is extremely fragile. Their climate combines tropical elements as a result of their position on the equator and temperate influences from the cold Humboldt Current. The islands are very dry and tropical forest is only to be found on the slopes; the coasts are often like steppe or desert. The first steps to protect the archipelago were taken in the 1950s and in 1959 Ecuador declared the region a national park.

The government's conservation agenda covers three areas: the eradication of animal varieties which have been introduced to the islands such as goats, rats, dogs, cats, pigs, and donkeys; the restoration of natural species by, for instance, breeding tortoises; and reducing as much as possible the damage caused by the rapid rise in tourism. This last goal is probably the most difficult, since visitors pour $100 million into the state exchequer every year, creating a precarious balance between ecological and economic interests.

A direct consequence of the tourism industry is migration from the mainland to the islands; some 14,000 people now live there, half of them in Puerto Ayora, and their numbers are growing. Five islands are inhabited. The permanent inhabitants are putting further strain on the scarce supply of fresh water largely because of their agricultural activities, are responsible for "waste nuisance" and increase the risk of fire. Because of intensive fishing the sea cucumber, a delicacy in Japanese cuisine, is in danger of extinction. When, at the end of 1994, the government announced a fishing ban, the fishermen began kidnapping researchers and rare turtles. Troops had to be brought in to restore order.

4   CULTURE: A SPANISH-INDIAN IDENTITY

Festivals

Festivals are an intrinsic part of Ecuador's social fabric, creating focal points for families and communities. Yet they often require huge financial sacrifices, especially if an individual is, according to tradition, designated *prioste*, the sponsor and organizer of a festival. When this happens, the prospect of saving up for a year or incurring debts can be a source of anxiety rather than pleasure. Angélica, who lives in the recently built *barrio* of "Comité del Pueblo" in Quito, has good cause not to attend any more church festivals:

> Just imagine that you have been appointed prioste, and you have to organize a festival that is even bigger than the last one. I really don't have that amount of money and it would mean getting deep into debt. It is better if I don't go, even though they have been badgering me all this year to go.

In spite of the difficulty which many Ecuadoreans experience in making ends meet, the festivals remain the highpoints of the year. Usually they are a mixture of Roman Catholic ritual and Indian traditions, most festivals coinciding with Christian feast days. One such instance of Christian-indigenous overlap is the festival of the solstice, the *Inti Raymi*, which was celebrated in the days of Inca rule on June 21. In the Otavalo region this event coincides with the feast of San Juan on June 24. The men especially dance until they drop, dressed in elaborate and bizarre costumes. By way of sacrifice to *Pacha Mama*, Mother Earth, fights are staged in which they pelt each other with stones.

Pase del niño

A central component of Christmas celebrations is the *pase del niño*, literally "passing on the child." The main theme is the adoration of the infant Jesus, and a figure of Jesus, often an antique dating from the colonial period, is to be found in almost every house. Tradition has it that being in possession of a Jesus figure will bring good luck, and every year the figure is "passed on" to other "godparents." Those who have the Jesus figure in their possession have the role of priostes and they are responsible for organizing the church festival. The most colourful is the pase del niño festival in Cuenca. According to local sociologist Susana Balarezo:

> It's easy to see that Cuenca is an area with a tradition of emigrating to the United States. Lots of children and adults show off their American clothing or their new cowboy boots at the pase del niño festival. The

Quechua fiesta, Riobamba *Tony Morrison/South American Pictures*

horses in the procession are decked out with dollars instead of sucres. It's incredible how many American presents and sweets are handed out to the children on the street.

On Christmas Eve all the Jesus figures are taken to the midnight mass to be blessed. Designating the priostes in the villages and districts is in itself cause for a big festival, and everybody has a specific role to play. The *mama negra*, for instance, is a man dressed as a black woman who dances through the streets, while the clowns, with the *payaso mayor*, the chief clown, at their head, mock all those they meet. Another important figure is the *curiquinue*, a mythical bird heralding the winter.

Fanesca and Good Friday

"*Hoy fanesca*," "fanesca today" can be seen written up in the windows of almost every restaurant during Holy Week. Fanesca is a traditional meatless soup in which twelve ingredients, symbolizing the twelve apostles, have been mixed and with which the Lenten fast is brought to an end. Opinions vary concerning the origin of the fanesca tradition. One popular belief holds that at the time Jesus was crucified Christians had to profess their faith underground and that they only came out of their hiding-place during Holy Week. And so they took all the food with them that they could get and mixed it all to make a rich soup for their meal. Fish, in the form of dried cod, is an essential ingredient of the soup, this according to some being because the Christians at that time were not allowed to wear a cross and therefore chose the fish as a symbol for Jesus. Another popular tradition relates that Mary was told that her son was to be crucified just as she happened to be cooking with a number of different cereals, and that the shock made her mix them all in the pan together.

Whatever its origin, the tradition of eating fanesca together with family, friends, and neighbors is still very much alive in modern Ecuador. Because all the ingredients have to be cooked separately, the preparation of fanesca is a highly intensive activity. As Angélica relates:

Before I begin making the soup I first ask all the members of the family and the neighbors whether they are also making fanesca this year. Those who aren't will get a little pan of soup from me because you really cannot have a Good Friday without it. One big problem is that the ingredients for fanesca have become more and more expensive. Above all it's the fish which is almost unaffordable just before Good Friday. That's why it's better to buy small pieces in the weeks before.

The economic problems confronting many Ecuadoreans are dramatically illustrated by this sort of complaint. In 1983 a family living on the minimum weekly wage of 5,000 sucres used up eight per cent of it on the preparation of fanesca; by 1994 this figure had risen to 28 per cent of the minimum wage, which at that time stood at 67,000 sucres.

Colada Morada and All Souls'

"*Angeles somos, pan queremos*," "we are angels and we want bread." Along the coast of Ecuador this is how little verse begins which greets the guests on All Souls' Day who visit families in which there has been a recent death. By way of honoring the dead the family opens its doors on this day to anybody who will come in and eat the dead person's favorite dish. Nor is the deceased's favorite drink forgotten, and before the guests leave, on their way to the next house, they have to drink three glasses of whatever was the preferred refreshment. They must also take a bag of bread with them.

Each region has its own way of honoring the dead. Every year on All Souls' Day, most households share *colada morada*, a syrupy drink made from flour or cornflour, mixed with all kinds of fruits such as blackberries, bilberries, pineapple, and *naranjilla* (a tropical fruit found only in Colombia and Ecuador). In the villages of the Andes people take this drink with them, together with bread shaped like dolls and other figures, when they go to the cemetery for a communal meal in the company of the dead.

Roast Guinea Pig

The centerpiece of every festival in the villages of the Sierra is a meal, and more often than not this is likely to consist of roast guinea pig or *cuy*, potatoes and peanut sauce. Guinea pigs, which run about the house loose until the feast day dawns, are considered a great delicacy but appeal less to foreign visitors. Drink, such as *chicha*, brewed from corn, lubricates the festivities, and sometimes ingenious games, like the *cuycuro* ritual, are played to push up the consumption of drink. After the guinea pigs have been eaten, a tiny bone from the ear, only a few tenths of an inch in size, is put on one side.

The host then places it in a glass of strong drink, preferably chicha or *canelazo*. The idea is to swallow the drink in one draught so that the tiny bone goes down with it, and the person who manages this may make a wish. It is, however, not as easy as it seems, as the greasy bone quickly sticks to the side of the glass. The next guest then tries his luck and so a good deal of alcohol is consumed before anybody is finally entitled to make a wish.

Music

A group of people moves slowly across the *páramo*; the musicians first, then the bride and groom, and after them the whole village, all following the music. In every village or barrio in Ecuador music is ever-present, accompanying all sorts of gatherings. Even in colonial times, visitors were struck by the musical skills of indigenous communities; as early as 1556 the Franciscan monk Fray Jodoco wrote that "Indians can learn to read and write with ease and they can play any instrument."

Two kinds of music are usually played at festivals, traditional Indian music and modern Spanish-European music, and the instruments used are those found throughout the Andes: the *quena* (bamboo flute), the *rondador* (pan pipes), the *maracas* (a rhythm instrument), the *charango* (a kind of ukulele introduced by the Spanish), *bombos* (drums), and the violin. Styles vary from place to place, and the music heard along the coast is very different from that in the Sierra. The most popular instrument among the black population of the coastal area is a huge wooden xylophone, the *marimba*. Guilleromo Ayoví, better known as Papá Roncón, is one of the best marimba players in the coastal village of Borbón (to the south of Valdés). He recalls how he decided to become a marimba player:

> It was a clear night and from my bedroom window I saw the moon kissing the top of a royal palm. Drawn by the brightness of the moonlight I ran down to the beach and what did I see there? I saw two angels going bim-bim, playing the marimba. I listened spellbound.

Sport

Every weekend the Parque Carolina, Quito's central park, is crowded with young city-dwellers who have come to relax, watch one another, and play sport. In a remote corner of the huge field two groups of somewhat older men stand in a row, each holding a board with big rubber studs. They are playing *pelota nacional*, literally "national ball," a game in which a small ball is hit back and forth between the two groups until a middle group succeeds in stopping it. Pelota nacional has had to struggle against a rather unfashionable image, and it is nowadays mostly older people who still play it.

Marathon, Santo Domingo
de los Colorados

*Edward Parker/South
American Pictures*

By far the most popular sports in Ecuador are soccer and volleyball. A *cancha*, a court of concrete or hardened earth the size of a large gymnasium, can be found everywhere in Ecuador, even in the remotest little hamlet. The game played here is a type of soccer, known strangely as *indoor*, and comprising two teams of six people. The other favorite is the more obviously named *ecua-volley*, a game played between two teams of three. According to ecuavolley rules, the net hangs at a height of at least six feet and players are allowed almost to catch the ball before throwing it over the net, a skill disallowed by orthodox volleyball. Enthusiastic spectators are frequently also players and national ecuavolley championships are organized.

Although many Ecuadoreans are sports enthusiasts, the country could claim few athletic achievements at international level until Jefferson Pérez won the first Ecuadorean gold medal at the Olympic Games in 1996. Ecuador enjoyed a brief spell of euphoria in 1993 when for the first time ever the national soccer team reached the semi-final of the Copa de América, the regional championships held that year in Ecuador. The 1996 defeat of Argentina was also cause for national celebrations. But even if Ecuador's own sportsmen are not top performers, the country can still support other Latin American countries, with the predictable exception of Peru. During the 1994 world cup Ecuador was distraught when neighboring Colombia was knocked out in the first round, but some regional pride was salvaged when Brazil subsequently won the championship.

The Writing on the Wall

No blank wall in Quito lasts long before being covered in graffiti. Unlike the mostly uninspiring messages of much British or U.S. graffiti, the writing on Ecuador's walls tends to be poetic, expressing sentiments such as: *es más fácil describir lo que no es amor,* "it's easier to describe what *isn't* love." For several years the young graffiti artists belonging to the group which signs its writings with a little sun and seagull have been roaming at

Anti-Peru and U.S. graffiti, Quito   *Paul Smith/PANOS Pictures*

night through the streets of Quito. Armed with aerosol cans, they provide the (as yet) unsullied walls with poetic and critical texts. The many graffiti poets, and the city has a wealth of them, belong to permanent groups, each with its distinctive "signature." Most of them come from the well-to-do middle class.

One anonymous would-be poet explains how the idea of self-expression through graffiti came about:

One afternoon I had met up with a group of friends. Some were feeling depressed, some were in love and others felt that they were not understood. If you want to publish your thoughts you can of course produce a magazine and then you'll find that nobody buys it, or you produce a radio program and nobody listens to it. It's better to paint graffiti because then you say what you think and you are not disappointed because nobody sees it.

The sun/seagull group specializes mainly in ecological messages, often spiced with a pinch of irony: *Menos mal que los ecologistas son biodegradables*, "fortunately environmental activists are biodegradable."

The first graffiti relating to the socio-economic crisis appeared in around 1991 and symptomized a widespread frustration, particularly in intellectual circles. Subsequently graffiti has spread relentlessly across the walls of Quito and has become an integral part of today's urban culture. The poetic and philosophical content of the early statements is now giving way increasingly to critical reflections on the social and economic situation. These slogans and messages have also entered the mainstream and are the subject of numerous articles, essays and dissertations; politicians regularly quote the graffiti which suit their purpose, while radio, television and the press discuss their significance.

Some messages are extremely transient and are wiped off again after a month, others remain in place much longer: "The government is like a local cinema, they get you in and then change the program"; or: Don't murder your ideals, they're a species threatened with extinction."

WHERE TO GO, WHAT TO SEE

Ecuador may be a relatively small country (about a quarter the size of Peru), but it boasts an impressive variety of landscapes and climates. It is claimed that you can canoe in the Amazon rainforest in the morning, cross the Andes in the afternoon, and swim in the tropical Pacific Ocean in the evening, although you would not be advised to try it. Added to the extraordinary natural variety is a rich culture, where indigenous influence is still alive and well, and some of Latin America's best preserved colonial architecture.

Nearly all visits to Ecuador start and end in the capital, Quito. The second highest capital city in Latin America (after La Paz), its altitude of nearly 10,000 feet may bring on *soroche* or mountain sickness in some visitors, but this usually short-lived. Compensation is to be found in its cool spring-like climate and dramatic scenery, comprised of snow-capped volcanoes and mountains. The old center offers the region's largest array of sixteenth-seventeenth-, and eighteenth-century colonial buildings, declared a World Heritage Site by UNESCO in 1978. Here the grandeur and wealth of colonial Quito are evident in the ornate houses, fine cloisters, and imposing public buildings.

The city's history as a religious center also lives on in its buildings, and no fewer than 86 churches are to be seen, the most sumptuous being the Jesuit church of La Compañía with its lavishly sculptured façade and interior. There are also several monasteries and convents. The main focal points are the Plaza Independencia, where the cathedral, archbishop's palace, and government palace are imposing monuments to sacred and secular power; the Plaza San Francisco, with the magnificent San Francisco church (carved ceiling, golden altar, art treasures); and the Plaza Santo Domingo, where a statue of José de Sucre points dramatically to the slopes of Pichincha where he defeated the Spanish army and ushered in independence. The street known as La Ronda is rich in steep cobbled streets, shady squares, and graceful arcades. Much has been tastefully restored in recent years, in contrast to the ugly road-dominated development of other parts of Quito, even if pickpockets and hordes of sidewalk vendors make the old center an unrelaxing place.

Those interested in colonial history should also make a point of visiting Cuenca, Ecuador's third largest city. Founded by the Spanish in 1557, it has a well-preserved area of cobbled streets and sixteenth-century buildings, many built with marble quarried nearby. Of particular architectural interest are the cathedral, the churches of San Blas and San Francisco, and the convent of La Concepción which dates from 1599.

Cathedral, Cuenca   *Kimball Morrison/*
South American Pictures

Quito has no shortage of museums, containing indigenous artefacts, exhibits from the independence period, and an impressive array of art. One of the most spectacular collections is to be found in the Guayasamín Museum, located in the north-easterly neighborhood of Bella Vista. The museum offers a panoramic view of the city, with Pichincha looming over it. Inside, there is an array of pre-colonial and colonial sculpture and artifacts together with work by Oswaldo Guayasamín, Ecuador's internationally celebrated painter. With Camilo Egas and Eduardo Kingman, Guayasamín is identified with the *indigenista* school of artists, who have graphically depicted indigenous Ecuador's struggle against oppression.

The country has several important archaelogical sites, where remains of pre-Conquest indigenous society have been discovered. Apart from Cochasquí (see p.43), one of the most fascinating displays of indigenous culture is to be found in a small museum at Agua Blanca, a village near the Machalilla National Park in the Pacific lowlands. Visitors can see ceramics dating from pre-Inca civilizations (c.AD1500) and can hire a guide to explore ruins nearby. Unlovely Guayaquil, not usually favored by tourists, also has several collections of gold items and other indigenous exhibits.

The most colorful – and most tourist-oriented – expression of modern-day indigenous life is the Saturday market at Otavalo. Bus-loads of *gringos* descend on the town, where there are three distinct market areas, devoted to livestock, fruit and vegetables, and textiles. Indian weavers from surrounding villages are the direct descendants of the indigenous textile-workers, forced by the Spanish to work in their *obrajes*. In nearby Peguche the remains of such a workshop can be visited, while local weavers produce ponchos and other clothes for the tourist market. Some travelers complain that Otavalo has become an expensive tourist-trap. Alternative markets, where a range of different indigenous communities sell their wares are: Zumbahua (Saturday), Pujilí (Sunday), Guamote (Monday), and Saquilisí (Thursday). Saquilisí is arguably the best market in Ecuador, full of color and cheaper than Otavalo.

A total of eighteen national parks and ecological reserves operate in the Sierra, Oriente, and coastal region. Near to Otavalo is the Cotacachi-Cayapas national park, where a five-hour walk takes you around a lake within a

Mountain path, Chimborazo   *Julio Etchart/Reportage*

volcanic crater. An unforgettable sight is the majestic Andean condor gliding overhead. More adventurous walkers may wish to climb one of the active volcanoes like Tungurahua near Baños, the more strenuous Cotopaxi, or the inactive Ilinizas, although proper equipment and a guide are essential.

Baños has recently developed a good reputation as a tourist center, and the town is a relaxing change from the hubbub of Quito and the squalor of Guayaquil. The site of supposedly therapeutic thermal baths, the town also has a statue of the Virgin in its Basilica which draws devout pilgrims from far and wide. Displays of discarded crutches testify to miracles performed by the Virgin. The town has a good selection of hotels and restaurants and enjoys a warm microclimate which is considerably more attractive than that of the nearby Sierra.

Eco-tourism is in vogue, and the main attraction is the Galápagos Islands, a unique and delicate eco-system some 600 miles west of the mainland. Its attractions include the legendary tortoises, the marine iguana, sealions and albatrosses. This is really for the serious naturalist and can be hugely expensive. A cheap alternative is the Isla de la Plata, only 15 miles offshore from Puerto López, where similar seabirds and flora can be observed.

One of eco-tourism's more laudable aims is to channel visitors' money into local communities. In Tena and Puyo, towns in the Oriente, it is possible – and recommended – to go with guides via small airplane into the Amazon jungle. These guides often belong to indigenous associations such as OPIP and Ricancie, which are active in conserving nature and local culture in an area under threat.

TIPS FOR TRAVELERS

Safety

Border skirmishes with Peru notwithstanding, Ecuador is a relatively peaceful country and has little military or paramilitary violence. Political demonstrations are commonplace in Quito and the security forces are quick to use teargas, so you are advised to avoid such confrontations.

Crime is a real problem, however, especially in Quito, Guayaquil, and some tourist sites. Particular crime black spots are La Ronda and Plaza San Francisco in the colonial center of Quito, the road up to the Pichincha volcano, large areas of Guayaquil and the beach at Atacames. In general bag-snatchers and pickpockets tend to prefer bus and train stations and crowded markets. It is best not to wear expensive watches or jewelry and to be very careful with cameras. Crime is much more frequent at night, and travelers should avoid bus stations and the poorer districts of cities after dark. You should carry your passport (or a photocopy of it) at all times.

Health

Malaria is endemic on the northwestern coast bordering Colombia and in large parts of the Oriente; precautions should be taken. Tap water is chlorinated, but it is wise to avoid it and opt for bottled water, especially as amoebic dysentery is a danger. Yellow fever is prevalent throughout Ecuador, and visitors should be vaccinated before going. Hepatitis is also reported to be commonplace. Other hazards include unhygienic restaurants and some of the world's worst drivers.

Soroche or altitude sickness affects many travelers. New arrivals in Quito and other high-altitude places should rest for a few days before attempting energetic climbing or other activities.

Women Travelers

Ecuador is a characteristically *macho* society, and single women are liable to experience some aspects of unwelcome male behavior. However, there are no particular dangers (other than those listed above) and most Ecuadoreans are kind and hospitable to all travelers.

Changing Money

There is little black market activity in Ecuador, but both banks and *cambios* offer variable exchange rates. There are many cash dispensers which can be used by travelers with some European and North American cash cards. Exchange desks in Ecuadorean banks often close at midday.

Souvenirs

The growth in tourism has spawned a large handicraft industry in Ecuador, some of which is of questionable quality. But much of what is on offer in the many markets around the country is good value for money. Otavalo is the best-known place for buying weavings and wall-hangings, while the market at Saquisilí is renowned for shawls, blankets, and embroidered garments.

Fewer crafts are to be seen in the coastal region, but this is where you can buy an authentic Panama hat. The best are reputed to be made in Montecristi, but other villages around Cuenca claim to produce superior hats. Other types of hat can be bought in the Sierra.

Ecuador also produces fine silver jewelry and a profusion of painted carvings, usually made from balsa wood.

Children

If health and security precautions are taken, children do not face any particular risks in Ecuador. Most locals are very friendly towards children.

Drugs

Although Ecuador is not by local standards a major drug producer, it is a transshipment point from Colombia and Bolivia into the U.S. and Europe. As a result, there is a good deal of marijuana and cocaine for sale. Coca is legal and can be bought from licensed vendors in markets who sell it as an antidote to *soroche*. It is advisable not to buy any illegal drugs in Ecuador, since penalties are harsh and prisons are far from comfortable.

ADDRESSES AND CONTACTS

Embassy of Ecuador
2535 15th Street, NW
Washington, D.C. 20009
U.S.A.
Tel: (202) 234-4744
Fax: (202) 745-0887 or
(202) 667-3482
E-mail:mecuawaa@pop.erols.com
Web site: www.ecuador.org/ecuador/
(includes all basic information)
special interest web sites:
www.ecuador.org/ecuador/ecotouri.htm
(eco-tourism)
www.ecuador.org/ecuador/travel (general
travel)

Ecuadorean Embassy,
3 Hans Crescent,
London SW1X 0LS, UK
Tel: 0171-584-1367
(provides tourist information)

Travel Agents/Tour Operators
Journey Latin America,
16 Devonshire Road,
London W4 2HD, UK
Tel: 0181-747-3108
(specialist travel agents)

Last Frontiers,
Swan House, High Street,
Long Crendon, Bucks HP18 9AF, UK
Tel: 01844-208405
(small group expeditions)

Alternative Travel Networks
South American Explorers Club,
126 Indian Creek Road,
Ithaca, NY 14850, U.S.A
Tel: 607-277-0488
(information and advice on travel to
the region)

South American Explorers Club,
Toledo 1254 y Luis Cordero, Quito
Tel: 566076
(library, bookstore, advice, and
information)

Ecuadorean Trade Centers

Miami Office
Doral Executive Park
3785 NW 82nd Avenue, #317
Miami, Florida 33166
Tel: (305) 716-5252
Web site: www.miamiweb.com.etc (in-
cludes website directory of Ecuador)

New York Office
399 Park Avenue, # 28B
New York, New York 10022
Tel: (212) 888-7277

FURTHER READING AND BOOKSTORES

Most relevant literature about Ecuador is in Spanish. This recommended further reading lists only books in English which are available in bookstores or good libraries.

Collinson, H (ed), *Green Guerrillas: Environmental Conflicts and Initiatives in Latin America and the Caribbean*, London, 1996.

Colyer, D., J. Alzamora, and R.L. Blumberg, *The Role of Agriculture in Ecuador's Development*, Washington, DC, 1990.

Corkill, D. and D. Cubitt, *Ecuador: Fragile Democracy*, London, 1988.

Darwin, C., *Voyage of the Beagle* (1839), London, 1989.

Goffin, A.M., *The Rise of Protestant Evangelism in Ecuador, 1895-1990*, Florida, 1994.

Isaacs, A., *Military Rule and Transition in Ecuador, 1972-92*, Basingstoke, 1993.

Kane, J., *Savages*, New York/London, 1996.

Martz, J.D., *Politics and Petroleum in Ecuador*, New Brunswick, 1987.

Mörner, M., *The Andean Past: Land, Societies, and Conflicts*, New York, 1985.

Perrottet, T (ed), *Ecuador: Insight Guide*, Singapore, 1993.

Pineo, R.F., *Social and Economic Reform in Ecuador: Life and Work in Guayaquil*, Florida, 1996.

FICTION
Icaza, J., *Huasipungo: The Villagers* (1934), Illinois, 1964.

Ortiz, A., *Juyungo* (1943), Washington, DC, 1982.

Vonnegut, K., *Galápagos*, New York/London, 1986.

LOCAL BOOKSTORES

Libri Mundi, Juan León Mera 851, Quito
Libro Express, Amazonas 816, Quito
Hotel Colón Internacional, Amazonas y Patria, Quito
Librería Cientifica, Luque 223 y Chile, Guayaquil

FACTS AND FIGURES

GEOGRAPHY

Official name: República del Ecuador (EC) (*ecuador =* equator)
Situation: between 1° 28' n and 5° s and 75° 12' and 81° 1' w; maximum north-south distance c.450 m., east-west c.400 m.; the Galápagos Islands lie c.600 m off the coast on the equator.
Surface area: 104,506 square miles (according to some sources 109,483 m″) including the Galápagos Islands (3,093 m″).
Administrative division: 21 *provincias*, divided into 183 *cantones* (cantons), divided

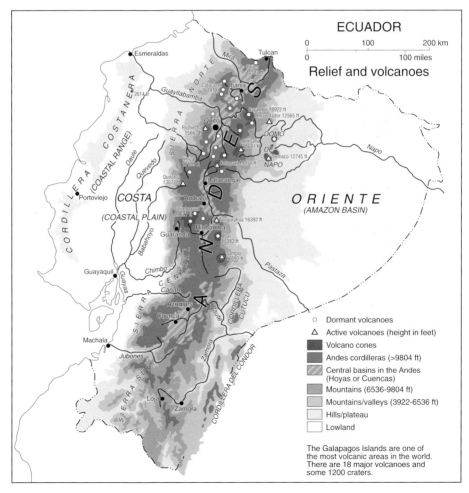

ECUADOR

Relief and volcanoes

| | 0 | 100 | 200 km |
| 0 | | 100 miles | |

○ Dormant volcanoes
△ Active volcanoes (height in feet)
▨ Volcano cones
▨ Andes cordilleras (>9804 ft)
▨ Central basins in the Andes (Hoyas or Cuencas)
▨ Mountains (6536-9804 ft)
▨ Mountains/valleys (3922-6536 ft)
▨ Hills/plateau
☐ Lowland

The Galapagos Islands are one of the most volcanic areas in the world. There are 18 major volcanoes and some 1200 craters.

76

into *parroquias* (parishes, municipalities).
Capital: Quito: population 1,282,000 (1990 census).
Other large towns (1990 population x 1000):
Guayaquil (1,664), Cuenca (227), Esmeraldas (136), Machala (166), Portoviejo (164).
Infrastructure: approx. 23,300 m. of road network, 4,200 m. asphalted and 18,700 m. metalled (1988); during the rainy season landslips occur regularly, blocking roads and sweeping away bridges; the *Panamericana* and the Quito-Santo Domingo-Guayaquil highway are the most important traffic arteries. An extensive network of private bus services and freight companies provides for road transport. The rail network covers only 602 m. and has lost much of its importance. The government is considering closing two of its three lines. International airports: Guayaquil and Quito; 208 smaller airfields, mostly landing strips in the Amazon region; Transportes Aéreos Militares Ecuatorianos (TAME), a commercial company belonging to the army, is the most important domestic airline, followed by Servicios Aéreos Nacionales (SAN) and Aerogal; another private company, the

Sociedad Ecuatoriana de Transportes Aéreos (SAETA), runs mainly international services. Main ports: Guayaquil, Esmeraldas, Manta, and Puerto Bolívar (Machala); oil ports: La Libertad and Balao; in the Amazon region the rivers Napo, Coca, and Pastaza are of great importance for transport. There are various pipelines for oil and natural gas transportation.
Relief, landscape, and climate: Ecuador is divided into three distinct ecological zones: the *Costa*, the coastal area (25%), the *Sierra*, the Andean highlands (24%) and the *Oriente*, the Amazon basin (49%); the Galápagos Islands form a separate fourth zone.
The western end of the *Costa* is covered by a low north-south mountain ridge (up to 2,600 feet) which at some points reaches as far as the sea. Between this Cordillera Costanera and the Andes lies a plain watered by the Babahoya, the Daule and their many tributaries. Shortly before the coast these form the Río Guayas which flows into the sea in a huge estuary. Guayaquil (average January temperature 81° F, average July temperature 76.1° F) lies on the Río Guayas. Between December and March, *el Niño*, a warm Gulf Stream

along the equator, brings heavy rainfall in the northern Costa, where tropical rainforest predominates. Towards the south this forest becomes drier tropical forest and savanna. The cold Humboldt stream coming from the south turns off to the west at the equator, meaning that the southern coastal regions are very dry (rainfall is sometimes only 3.9 inches). In the surrounding steppe-like regions a vegetation prevails which includes the characteristic *ceibo*, a tree with a bottle-shaped trunk. The **Sierra** consists of an eastern and a western mountain range, the *Cordilleras*, with many peaks higher than 13,000 feet Between them lies a chain of basins at a height of 5,200 to 9,800 feet *(cuencas* or *hoyas)* which together form the extensive *Depresión Interandina*. The total breadth of the Sierra is between 25 and 45 m. There are a number of volcanoes in the two Cordilleras; the highest are the inactive Chimborazo (20,700 feet), Cayambe and El Altar, and the active Cotopaxi (19,340 feet), Tungurahua, Antizana, and Sangay. The German geographer Alexander von Humboldt, who visited the country in the nineteenth century, christened the road through the depression The

"Volcano Avenue." In the northern Sierra volcanic activity is of more recent date than in the south. Most of the basins and the adjoining slopes have a moderate climate (Quito: average January temperature 58.6° F, average July temperature 56.6° F); daily temperature fluctuations can be considerable; night frost is normal in August and September. The Costa and Amazon flanks of the Cordilleras are covered with humid tropical Andean forest or tropical mountain forest in which characteristic trees *(quiñua* and *quishuar)*, bromelias and orchids grow. Between 11,800 and 13,100 feet, in most of the basins and on the adjoining slopes, *páramo* vegetation prevails with grasslands, low bushes, and remnants of Andean forest. Above this, vegetation becomes sparse and at altitudes higher than about 15,750 feet there is only permanent snow. From north to south the principal *hoyas* are: the Hoya del Mira (near Ibarra, mostly under 6,500 feet) with a warm, dry climate and a natural vegetation with succulents and cacti dominating; the Hoya de Guayllabamba (Quito), surrounded by an impressive complex of volcanoes and enjoying a moderate climate; the Hoya de Pastaza, a plain running

north-south (moderate climate), and seismically extremely active (Ambato, Latacunga, and Riobamba have on a number of occasions been destroyed by earthquakes and lava-flows); the Pequeña Hoya del Cañar and the Hoya del Paute are less defined than those in the north because they have been filled in by lava-flow; in the extreme south, in the province of Loja, the contours are very steep with small valleys.

In the **Amazon region (Oriente)** there is a third *cordillera*, parallel to the Andes, running north-south and comprising the Domo de

Napo, the Cordillera del Cutucú, and the Cordillera del Cóndor. This is a seismically very active region. By far the greater part of Amazonia consists of a plain running down from west to east with sedimentary deposits brought by the rivers flowing from the Andes. The region is covered with tropical rainforest and forms a small part of the great Amazonian rainforest. The average temperature is 77° F and all the year round (particularly in May-December) there is heavy rainfall (120-150 inches annually).

Galápagos Islands consist of thirteen large and a number of smaller islands, all of volcanic origin. The highest point is the Cerro Azul (5,540 feet) on the island of Isabela, more than 14,800 feet when measured from the sea-bed. Together with erosion caused by the sea, volcanic activity has given rise to a number of peculiar landscape formations. Although the islands lie on the equator there is considerable variation in the weather according to the season: from June to December there are strong winds and the temperature fluctuates between 64° and 68° F; September and October have heavy rainfall; from January to May the temperature lies between 75° and 82° F and tropical downpours occur regularly. On most of the islands the vegetation is desert-like on the coast and consists of dry tropical forest on the highest parts of the volcano slopes.

Best tourist season: June to September inclusive: dry in the Andes and not too hot on the coast; Galápagos: January to June inclusive.

POPULATION

Population (1996): 11 million (1990 census: 9.6 million).
Annual population growth: 1970-1980: 2.9%, 1980-1992: 2.5%.
Population density (1993): 106 inhabitants per m".
Urbanization (1992): 58%; annual growth of urban population: 4%.
Fertility: in the 1970s an Ecuadorean woman had an average of 6.9 children; in 1990 that figure had dropped to 4.4.
Age structure (1991): 0-14: 39.5%, 15-64: 56.9%; 65+: 3.6%.
Birthrate (1992): 29 per 1,000.
Mortality rate (1992): 7 per 1,000.
Infant mortality (1992): under 1 year of age: 45 per 1,000.
Average life expectancy (1992): 66.1 years, men 64 years and women 68 years.
Doctors (1992): 1 doctor per 820 inhabitants.
Daily per capita calorie consumption (1991): 2,047.
Illiteracy (1990): 14%; rural: 17.4%, urban: 4.9%; 60% of all illiterates are women;

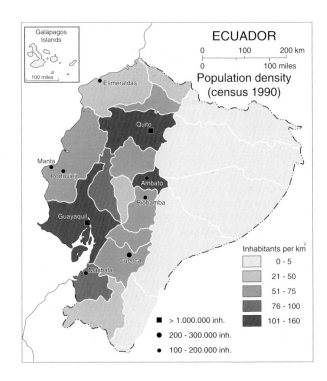

Galapagos Islands

100 miles

ECUADOR

0   100   200 km
0   100 miles

Population density
(census 1990)

Esmeraldas
Quito
Manta
Portoviejo
Ambato
Riobamba
Guayaquil
Cuenca
Machala

Inhabitants per km²

☐	0 - 5
☐	21 - 50
☐	51 - 75
☐	76 - 100
☐	101 - 160

■ > 1.000.000 inh.
● 200 - 300.000 inh.
● 100 - 200.000 inh.

coastal region: 9%, Sierra: Chimborazo 23%, Cotopaxi 20%, Bolívar 19%, Cañar 18%. *Education (1990):* 87% of children aged between 6 and 11 attend school; 12-19 years of age: 60%; 19-24 years of age: 24%; of the population over the age of 24, 44% have had primary *(primario)*, 23% secondary *(secundario)*, and 13% higher *(superior)* education; in 1992 2.7% of GDP was spent on education. *Universities (1988):* 20 universities and 3 technical colleges (16 state and 7 private); c. 50% of the 190,000 students study in Quito and Guayaquil. *Social development index:* (UNDP Human Development Index 1993): 74th position (category "middle"); UK 10th, U.S. 6th position; total 173 positions. *Ethnic composition (1990):* mestizo 55%; indigenous people 25% (main peoples: Quichuas, Shuar, Ashuar, Huaorani, Siona-Secoya, Cofán, Chachi, Tsachila, Awa); whites 10%, and blacks 10%. *Religion:* 96% Roman Catholic (19% combine this Catholicism with animism); 2% Protestant. *Languages:* Spanish; all Indian communities have their own language (most widespread: Quichua) but mostly also speak Spanish.

HISTORY AND POLITICS

Key historical dates: 3500 BC: earliest agricultural settlement of the Valdivias * 500-1400 AD: various flourishing Indian kingdoms on the coastal plain, the Sierra, and the Oriente * 1460: Tupac Yupanqui begins northward expansion of Inca kingdom * 1526: the Spaniard Bartolomé Ruiz lands on the coast near the present-day town of Esmeraldas * 1530: end of the struggle between Atahualpa and Huascar for the Inca kingdom * 1532: Pizarro conquers Cajamarca and captures Atahualpa * 1534: capture of Quito * 1563: foundation of Audiencia Real de Quito * 1810: uprising and bloodbath in Quito during the struggle for independence * 1822: General Sucre defeats the Spanish army in the Battle of Pichincha * 1822-1830: Ecuador a member of the Federation of Gran Colombia * 1830: independence * 1832: Ecuador annexes the Galápagos Islands * 1858-1860: war with Peru; loss of substantial part of Amazon territory * 1869-1875: Gabriel García Moreno establishes a theocratic government * 1895-1912: "Liberal Revolution" under Eloy Alfaro * 1933 Velasco Ibarra elected for first of five times * 1941: Peruvian troops occupy the southern part of the country * 1942: the frontier between Ecuador and Peru is provisionally established in the Rio de Janeiro Protocol * 1963-1966: military dictatorship * 1964: land reform act * 1967: first oil finds in the Amazon basin * 1972-1979: military dictatorship * 1979: return to democracy; new constitution; death of Velasco Ibarra * 1984-1988: "Andean Thatcherism" of León Febres Cordero * 1987: earthquake destroys main oil pipeline * 1990: Indian uprising * 1992: Ecuador leaves OPEC * January 1995: border conflict with Peru * July 1996: presidential victory of Abdalá Bucaram * February 1997: Bucaram forced out of office; Fabián Alarcón becomes interim president. *Constitution/administration:* presidential republic; the president (period of office 4 years) appoints the members of the cabinet and the provincial governors;

presidential elections in two rounds. The parliament *(Congreso Nacional* or *Cámara Nacional de Representantes)* has 82 members (as from 1996); 12 are elected in national elections for 4 years and 70 are elected in provincial elections for 2 years.
Head of State: Abdalá Bucaram, since August 1996; presidents since 1979: Jaime Roldós Aguilera 1979-1981, Osvaldo Hurtado Larrea 1981-1984, León Febres Cordero 1984-1988, Rodrigo Borja Cevallos 1988-1992, Sixto Durán Ballén 1992-1996.
Political parties (number of seats in Congress as from August 1996): *Partido Social Cristiano* (PSC) 27, *Partido Roldosista Ecuatoriano* (PRE) 19, *Democracia Popular* (DP) 12, *Movimiento Pachakutik – Nuevo País* (6), *Izquierda*

Democrática (ID) 5, *Movimiento Popular Democrático* (MPD) 4; other parties share nine seats.
Armed forces (1994): 57,800; ground forces: 50,000; navy: 4,800; airforce: 3,000.
Military expenditure as a percentage of combined spending on education and healthcare (1991). 40%.
Membership of international organizations: UN and UN organizations, OAS (Organization of American States), IDB (Inter-American Development Bank), Pacto Andino (free-trade zone of Andean countries Bolivia, Colombia, Ecuador, Venezuela), ALADI (Association for Latin American Integration), SELA (Latin American Economic System), ICO (International Coffee Organization), Group of 77 (Organization of Developing

Countries), Organization of Non-Aligned Countries.
Media and communication (1990): 32 radios, 8 television sets, and 5 telephones per 1,000 inhabitants (UK/U.S. 1,146/2,123 radios, 435/815 television sets, 477/789 telephones per 1,000 inhabitants). Daily newspapers. 36, of which 8 important; in Quito: *El Comercio* (130,000), *Hoy* (55,000), *El Tiempo* (35,000), and *Ultimas Noticias* (90,000);in Guayaquil: *Expreso* (30,000), *La Razón* (28,000), *El Telégrafo* (35,000), *El Universo* (174,000); most important weekly newspaper: *Vistazo.* Newspaper publishers, radio and television stations are more than 90% privately-owned; 324 radio stations, some also broadcasting in Quichua; 16 television stations, 10 with a national network.

ECONOMY

Unit of currency: sucre; (exchange rate per $1 3,130 (1996); 1,919 (1993); 1,046 (1991)
Inflation: 1995: 22.9%; 1994: 25.4%; 1987-1993: 54%, 1980-1992: 40%, 1970-1980: 14% (annual average).
Gross Domestic Product (GDP): US$28.8 billion (1993).

Per capita GDP (1993): US$1,170
Private cars per 1,000 inhabitants: 34
Economic growth: 1970-1980: 9.5%; 1980-1992: 2.3%; 1991: 5%; 1992: 3.5%; 1993: 2%; 1994: 4.4%; 1995: 2.3%
Foreign debt (1996): US$16 billion.
Foreign debt as percentage of export of goods and

services (1995): 240%.
Development aid per inhabitant (1991): US$20.4; in 1991 Ecuador received US$60.9 million in grants and US$122.8 million in loans from the European Union.
Structure of the economy, share of GDP (1995): agriculture 12%, industry 21%, petroleum and mining 10.5%, construction 4.5%, services 26.4%, other 25.6%.